NORTHERN HAITI:
Land, Land Use, and Settlement

NORTHERN HAITI:

LAND, LAND USE, AND

SETTLEMENT

A Geographical Investigation of
the Département du Nord

Harold A. Wood

UNIVERSITY OF TORONTO PRESS

Acknowledgments

THE AUTHOR wishes gratefully to acknowledge the invaluable assistance provided in the execution of this research by the following:

Dr. D. F. Putnam, Head, Department of Geography, University of Toronto, whose constructive criticism has been much appreciated.

McMaster University, which provided financial assistance during the initial and final stages of the research.

The Social Science Research Council of Canada, which provided financial assistance during the intermediary stages of the research.

The government of Haiti, which provided transportation in the field and assisted the writer in other ways too numerous to mention.

The Service Interaméricain Coöpératif de Production Agricole, which provided the author with living accommodation and transportation in the St. Raphaël area.

M. André Auguste, of the Haitian Department of Public Works, who, as chauffeur to the author, served with efficiency, diligence, and devotion.

His parents, Rev. and Mrs. A. Groves Wood, formerly of Cap Haitien, Haiti, who provided living accommodation in the field, and whose support in other tangible and intangible ways has been indispensable.

His wife, without whose willingness to forego much, this study could not have been undertaken.

The people of Haiti, whose courtesy, hospitality, and cheerfulness in the face of difficulties indicate that they cherish values which make them one of the truly civilized people of the earth.

Publication of this work has been made possible through a grant from the Social Science Research Council of Canada, using funds provided by the Canada Council, and assistance from the Publications Fund of the University of Toronto Press.

H.A.W.

Contents

Plates, Maps, and Diagrams

Introduction

ANY SECTION of the earth's surface has different meanings for different people. To the geologist, it represents an assemblage of rocks and recent unconsolidated deposits. The sociologist things of it primarily as the home of people, whose values, attitudes, and relationships are worthy of study for their own sake. The economist is interested in the ramifications of the act of exchange; the political scientist in the acts of power and control. Each one focuses his attention on some aspect of the territory and then, consciously or unconsciously, considers this aspect in its world-wide manifestations. Thus various academic disciplines study the earth, each from its own point of view, seeking not a full understanding of any area, but specific principles or laws of global application.

The geographer, too, looks at the world and its parts with a point of view, but one which is based on the concept of the unity or wholeness of the landscape. While fully recognizing the value of extracting for study a single item or items, he also realizes that such an extraction is, in some respects, a violation of reality. Rocks and men, food and laws, do not exist in isolation one from another, but in a union imposed by the bounds of finite space. Nor is the union fortuitous; its elements are linked by countless causal connections. Even man and his works, despite the apparent freedom of human choice, are not immune from influences which, for their very subtlety, require detailed and careful consideration.

Yet even geography does not normally embrace every phenomenon on the surface of the earth. Some elements, such as the distance to the earth's centre, may be considered as constant, except in such peripheral realms as cartography and geophysics. Others, such as human blood types, may display variations from place to place, yet they are variations which have little apparent relation with anything else. Elements such as these are omitted in virtually all geographical studies.

The process of selectivity, which begins in this rather objective fashion, then becomes more subjective. Some geographers, interested primarily in physical phenomena, confine their attention to the inter-relations among rocks, climate, soil, plants, and animals. Others, more concerned with human factors, limit themselves to a consideration of the distribution of man, his activities, his habitations, and his other constructions.

Nevertheless, the subjectivity of the process of selection is influenced in many cases by the nature of the area which is being studied. Even the geographers who deal with the interrelations between the physical and cultural environments—and they constitute the bulk of the members of the profession—cannot always give equal emphasis to both sets of phenomena. For example, in many of the more highly developed regions of the world, human initiative has been such that minor differences in landforms, soils, and climate are scarcely reflected in the distribution of man and the character of his economic activities. Here, only in the broad perspective is it possible to appreciate the influence of the physical environment upon human affairs, and detailed geographical investigations will frequently lay stress upon an examination of economic, political, or social factors.

In many undeveloped and thinly populated regions, on the other hand, the links between man and nature are so direct that they may be fairly obvious and recognizable as a result of merely cursory examination. In such areas it is the unravelling of the web of relationships between the various elements of the physical environment taken alone which often comprises the most challenging task of the geographer.

There remain, however, large and important territories which lie between these two extremes. In these places neither man nor nature has clearly the upper hand, and the relations between them are close and direct, though complex and often misunderstood. The best examples of such areas may be found in densely populated parts of the humid tropics, where, without machinery and with only simple tools, men obtain from the land the food they eat, the materials from which they make their homes and furniture, and some items which can be sold to provide a cash income.

For these peasant farmers, nature is at once an easy mistress and a hard taskmaster. Within certain limitations, the necessities of life are not difficult to obtain. With relatively little prodding, the earth will produce considerable quantities of grain, vegetables, fruits, roots, and timber. Provided that the amount of land available per capita is sufficient, hunger is at worst seasonal or local.

Yet, in many areas, populations have increased until their demands

on the land exceed its productive capacity. In this situation, the limits
of productivity attract more attention than the levels of productivity.

It is true, of course, that limits of productivity are not peculiar
to tropical lands. The barriers, however, are more difficult to push
back in the tropics than in other parts of the world for reasons that
are both physical and human. In the physical realm, excessive heat,
droughts, and torrential rains pose problems which have thus far defied
solution. In the human realm, disease, cultural breakdown, and political
subservience have stifled initiative. Hence the agricultural revolution
which was the *sine qua non* of economic progress in temperate lands
has proved to be impossible to export to the tropics except in a very
limited way. Peasant farmers, their numbers growing, find that their
survival, let alone their material progress, demands that they increase
agricultural yields or turn to non-agricultural occupations. Yet both
these courses of action involve the surmounting of seemingly impassable barriers.

The problem is not a new one, but at the present time it is more
serious than ever before. Migration is seldom now a feasible solution,
and, as spreading hygiene reduces death rates, there is insufficient
time for new techniques to be discovered by the old method of trial
and error. Consequently in many tropical lands there is a need for
development to be guided. Guidance, in turn, should be based on a
knowledge of all the factors involved, not the least of these being the
quality of the land and the ways in which this quality is reflected in
its use.

It is to contribute to this knowledge that the present study has been
undertaken. The area selected for investigation is the most densely
populated département in the most densely populated country of Latin
America. Here it is possible to observe something very close to the
maximum productivity possible, under primitive techniques, in a variety
of types of land. Here, therefore, the barriers which limit man's further
progress may be seen at particularly close range. Here, too, is a standard
which helps one to judge the true severity of population pressure in
other areas of similar structure and climate.

As a geographical laboratory, the Département du Nord has the additional advantage of possessing racial and cultural homogeneity, but
marked geologic, topographic, and climatic contrasts. Hence the influences of the physical environment stand out with unusual clarity, and
their variety makes possible a wide application in other parts of the
American tropics of the knowledge obtained here.

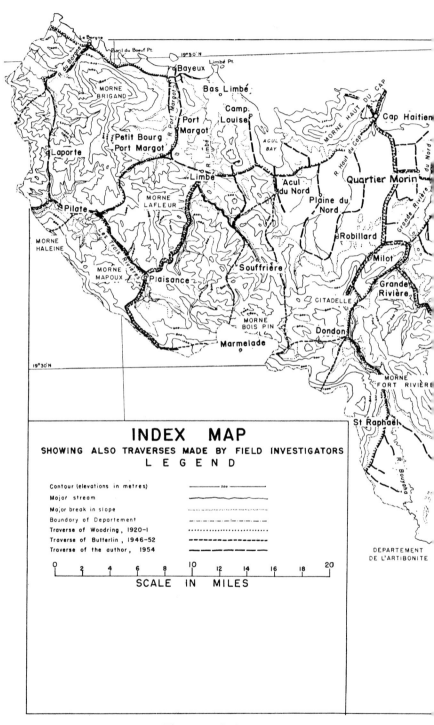

Figure 1.   Index Map

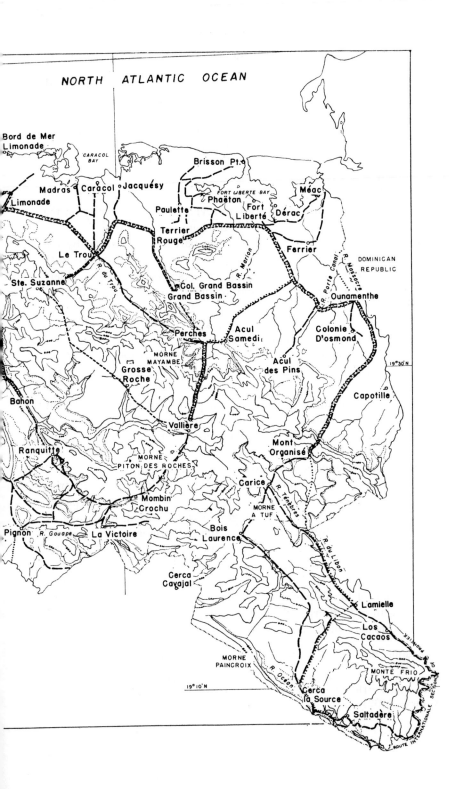

INTRODUCTION

PROCEDURE

Prior to the execution of the present study, the Département du Nord, Republic of Haiti, was a relatively little known area. Only two systematic studies had been carried out in the field, both having to do with the geology of the Département, and both dealing with the Département only as a part of the country as a whole. The initial investigation was carried out by Wendell P. Woodring, John S. Brown, and Wilbur S. Burbank[1] of the United States Geological Survey in 1920 and 1921. Subsequently, between 1946 and 1952, Professor Jacques Butterlin,[2] of the Institut Français in Port-au-Prince, undertook to revise the earlier survey on the basis of additional field traverses and in the light of topographic information contained in a series of maps covering part of Haiti issued by the United States Army Map Service in 1948 on a scale of 1:50,000. Both surveys, however, were of a reconnaissance type; traverses were widely spaced (Figure 1), and information recorded for areas not directly observed was largely subjective. Although Haiti had been covered in large part by vertical aerial photographs taken in 1942 and 1944 by the United States Army, there is no indication that Butterlin made direct use of the photographs in preparing his map of the geology of Haiti, though, as indicated above, he did use maps prepared from some of the photographs.

Apart from a climatological study of Hispaniola,[3] therefore, relevant published material available to the author of the present report comprised, in essence, a generalized geologic account and topographic maps on a scale of 1:50,000 covering approximately 44.5 per cent of the total area of the Département. However, through the co-operation of the governments of Haiti and the United States, prints of these aerial photographs were obtained, covering about 92 per cent of the Département. Using these as a source of topographic information, and using as horizontal ground control the position of the four trigonometric stations lying within the area in question, plus various measurements made by him in the field, the writer drew up, by the radial line method, planimetric maps on the 1:50,000 scale for the previously unmapped southeastern section of the Département. These maps were then reduced and combined with reductions of the U.S. Army maps to produce a base for the detailed maps which accompany this report.

[1]Woodring, Brown, and Burbank, *Geology of the Republic of Haiti* (Port-au-Prince, 1924).

[2]Butterlin, *Géologie de la République d'Haiti* (Port-au-Prince, 1954).

[3]Leo Alpert, "The Climate of Hispaniola" (Clark University, Worcester, Mass., M.A. thesis, 1939).

Investigation of soil and land use characteristics was carried out during the months May to August, 1954, in field traverses which are recorded cartographically in Figure 1. Classifications of soils and land use were then devised such that individual categories were geographically significant and also identifiable on the aerial photographs. Through interpretation of these photos the detailed maps were then drawn up. Chemical and physical analyses of fifty-six soil samples were carried out in the laboratories of the Département de l'Agriculture of the Republic of Haiti in Port-au-Prince. An additional fifty-seven samples were analysed chemically in the Department of Geography, McMaster University, Hamilton, Ontario.

In the two narrow strips of territory for which aerial photography was not available, the information recorded will be correct only in general outline. Both these strips, however, lie across areas of physiographic uniformity and relatively low population. Hence, any errors made here will be of little significance, either in terms of location or with respect to the conclusions reached.

NORTHERN HAITI:
Land, Land Use, and Settlement

1. The Broad Perspective

Size and Location

The Département du Nord occupies approximately 4,100 square kilometres (1,583 square miles), or 15 per cent of the area of the Republic of Haiti (see Figure 2). It is bounded on the west by the Département du Nord-Ouest, on the south by the Département de l'Artibonite, on the east by the Dominican Republic and on the north by the Atlantic Ocean. The Département lies wholly within the tropics, extending latitudinally from 19° 06′ 01″ N. to 19° 52′ 59″ N. Its longitudinal limits are 71° 38′ 42″ W. and 72° 37′ 30″ W.

Relief

The Département includes sections of the major mountain range, the largest coastal lowland, and the most extensive interior plateau of Hispaniola. Approximately 60 per cent of the Département is within the mountain chain known in Haiti as the Massif du Nord and in the Dominican Republic as the Cordillera Central. Within the Département this range is not high, for no peaks exceed 3,800 feet in elevation, but much of it is intricately dissected and very rugged. Geologically it is fairly complex and includes sedimentary, magmatic, and plutonic rocks (Figure 3).

The northeastern 35 per cent of the Département lies within a broad trough which, in the Dominican Republic, extends between the Cordillera Central and the Cordillera Septentrional. In that country this depression is known as the Cibao Valley; its extension into Haiti is referred to as the Plaine du Nord. This plain too is fairly complex, being in part a plain of abrasion and in part a plain of deposition.

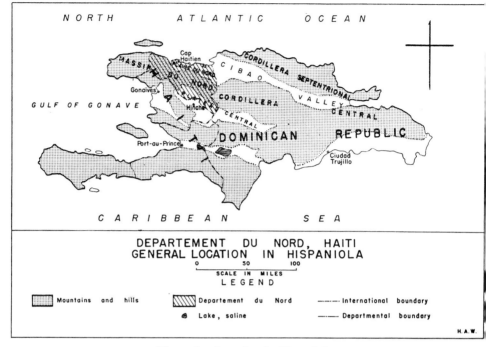

Figure 2. Location in Hispaniola

Five per cent of the Département, in its south-central section, is a slightly dissected plain, about 1,000 feet above sea level, comprising a portion of the Central Plateau of Haiti.[1] Sediments, both consolidated and unconsolidated, form the surface of the plateau.

Climate[2]

Tropical temperatures prevail throughout the Département with mean values ranging from 78°F. on the coast to 68°F. on the highest peaks. The mean annual temperature range is nowhere greater than 9°F.

The amount of precipitation, however, varies considerably from place to place within the Département, the lowest recorded annual mean rainfall being 34.23 inches and the highest 81.16 inches. In general, the hills receive more rainfall than the plains, the heaviest precipitation falling on the northern ranges of the mountains; southwards a rain-shadow effect becomes progressively more pronounced. To some extent also, the entire eastern part of the Département falls under the rain-shadow of

[1]Harold A. Wood, "Stream Piracy in the Central Plateau of Hispaniola," *The Canadian Geographer*, no. 8, 1956.

[2]Leo Alpert, "The Climate of Hispaniola."

the Cordillera Septentrional of the Dominican Republic. Consequently there is also a reduction in precipitation from west to east.

Thunderstorms account for the bulk of the spring and summer precipitation, and hurricanes contribute large but irregular amounts in the fall. Winter rain is associated with the passage of weak cyclonic depressions or is orographic in character. The northeast facing slopes of the mountains receive more rain in winter than in summer, but, for the remainder of the Département, winter is a relatively dry season.

Drainage

The Département contains an intricate network of streams, some draining into the Gulf of Gonave, though nearly three-quarters of the drainage is towards the Atlantic. Except near their headwaters, most of the streams in the mountains are permament. The larger ones are also permanent in the plains, though during the dry season the water of smaller streams is frequently dissipated by evaporation and percolation before it reaches the sea. All streams are subject to great fluctuations in level and none are navigable.

Natural Vegetation

It is not possible to present a precise picture of the original vegetation of the Département since there are few, if any, places in which it has not been disturbed. Nevertheless, it is safe to say that the mountains and the more humid parts of the northern plain were forested. Much of the forest was of the tropical, semi-deciduous type, though extensive coniferous stands were found in the hills of the southeast, and mangroves lined much of the coast.

Drier sections of the Plaine du Nord had a cover consisting largely of xerophytic forest with some stretches in which trees were confined to the margins of watercourses, the interfluves being areas of open grassland. Somewhat similar vegetation was found in that section of the Central Plateau which lies within the Département, though the grassland in most places was not open. Instead it was dotted throughout by scattered trees, mostly semi-deciduous but including some conifers.

Soils

The Département contains soils of both the lateritic and the margalitic types. Throughout most of the areas of low relief, except in zones of very recent alluviation or emergence, distinct soil profiles are to be observed. In the mountains, however, erosion has destroyed all but a few remnants of such mature soils as might have existed.

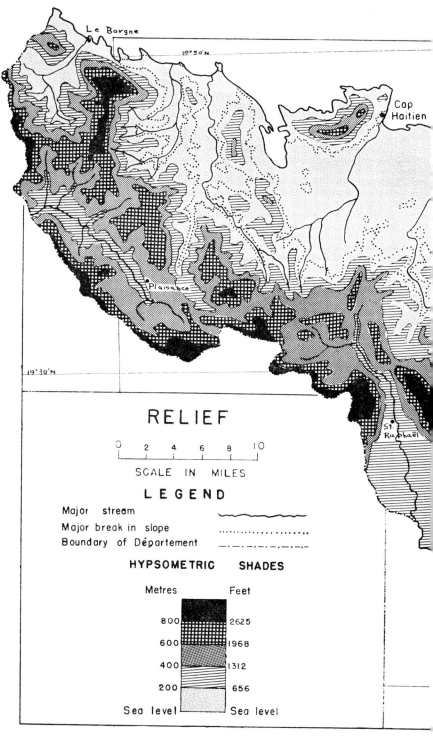

RELIEF

0   2   4   6   8   10
SCALE IN MILES

LEGEND

Major stream
Major break in slope
Boundary of Département

HYPSOMETRIC SHADES

Metres		Feet
800		2625
600		1968
400		1312
200		656
Sea level		Sea level

Figure 3.   Relief

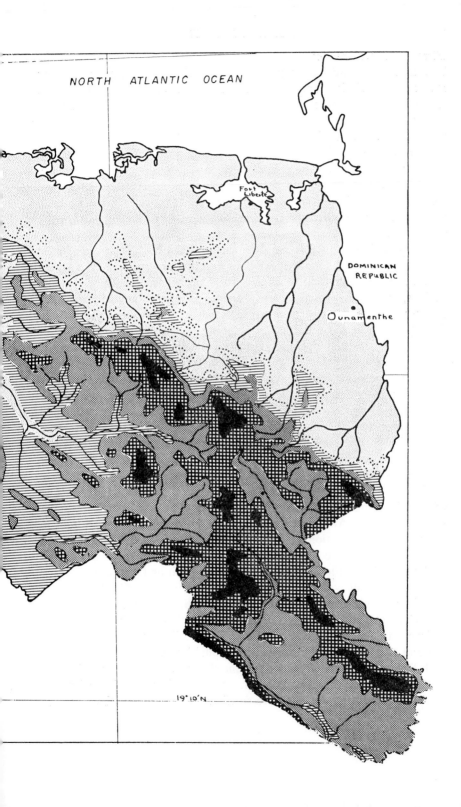

NORTH ATLANTIC OCEAN

Fort
Liberté

DOMINICAN
REPUBLIC

Ounamenthe

19°10'N

Historical Development

The history of Haiti has been one of political and economic revolution rather than evolution. In pre-Columbian days the Arawak Indians were exterminated by Caribs advancing from the east and they, in their turn, were virtually eradicated as a result of the conquest of western Hispaniola first by the Spanish, then by the French. One very seldom finds in Haiti any trace of its former Indian inhabitants, except that ancient artifacts are unearthed here and there, and occasionally one sees an individual with features and colouring which suggest a trace of Indian blood. On the whole the culture of the Arawaks and Caribs is dead, although a few traits are preserved in the use made of certain plants such as manioc.

European interest was focused on the production of sugar cane in the northern plain, and to provide labour for this enterprise Negro slaves were imported from Africa. But as the Europeans had wiped out the Indians, so in time did the Negroes erase from the land almost every visible vestige of European occupation. Rising in revolt at the turn of the eighteenth century, the slaves not only massacred or expelled their former white masters but also destroyed the inanimate symbols of the system which had enslaved them. Of the scores of palatial plantation houses, scarcely one escaped the torch. Towns were burned and pillaged. Cane fields were set ablaze. The land was scarcely recognizable.

When the orgy was over, life began anew for the Negroes, who had now become the only ones really entitled to be called Haitians. But it was a new kind of life. No longer could sugar cane be the major crop since there was no organization to produce or market the sugar. No longer was there an establishment to maintain irrigation works. No longer were good roads needed. No longer had the old property boundaries any validity. No longer was it necessary to live in the plains, where the sugar estates had been. And so the people scattered to seize land and hold it. They pre-empted sections of the plain; they moved into the valleys and hills. Wherever they could find land which seemed capable of producing food crops, they settled and built their tiny thatch and wattle huts.

The movement was never organized. Governments existed, but they were far removed from the scene, and their influence on the peasant was generally light and indirect. Those administrations which attempted to achieve an effective control were overthrown. Freedom was something real and precious: freedom on an individual basis, with its roots in the land. Dispersed rural settlement became the rule, each family in its own small holding, for there was no title to the land except that of actual occupation and use. Villages were small and far apart, for there was no important function for them to fulfil. No external enemies made it necessary to congregate for defence. Religion required no communal centres of worship, for it was mainly a matter of the relations between a family[3] and its traditional spirits. Trade was too limited, in total amount and in the variety of goods exchanged, to nourish commercial towns.

Thus a biracial community was replaced by one overwhelmingly black. A commercial economy, with its rich and its poor, gave way to one of subsistence, in which the resources of the land were shared more or less equally by all.

The century and a half which have since elapsed have produced remarkably few changes. True, the population has greatly increased, and with congestion has come immobility, but the basic social order and the approach to living remain unaltered. Like primitive people everywhere, the Haitian peasant seeks food, home, and dignity. In common with countless others, his grasp on the first of these necessities is sometimes tenuous. Yet, unlike many, he clings firmly to the last two. The individual refuses to give up his freedom, even though, in the two aspects of life which are closest to him—his family and his land—he is still outside the law. Of the domestic unions in the Département as a whole, only one in four, and in some rural areas only one in ten, is recognized by the state as a legal marriage. In the field of land tenure the position of the peasant is even more irregular. No general cadastral survey has ever been executed, so that even those few individuals who possess some kind of "deed" to their land have no way of legally establishing the location of their property. The livelihood and position of a man still ultimately depend on the free recognition of his claims by his fellows.

It is, perhaps, to be expected, and in any case it is true, that here, where the importance of the individual is supreme, one finds also a keen recognition of the rights and privileges of others and of the value of co-operation in the community. The practical application of this quality is best seen in the organization of voluntary work parties in which the peasants, with mirth and song, clear a field or erect a house for one of their number with no reward other than a meal and the knowledge that the favour will on request be returned. It is also a rewarding experience to travel through the Haitian countryside. The friendship and courtesy with which the stranger is greeted are not frequently encountered elsewhere, even among peoples which we are pleased to call more civilized.

Consequently the chief legacy of the past in the geography of the Département du Nord, and, to a considerable extent in other parts of

[3]The Haitian family is patrilineal and patrilocal, normally monogamic though occasionally polygynous, and is of the restricted type.

Haiti as well, has been the creation of a free dispersed peasantry, so homogeneous in its background and in its philosophy of life that these factors need not be considered as variables affecting the use of the land.

The cultural contribution of the French has, however, been a major one. French legal, administrative, and educational patterns are followed. French is the official language, while the language of the people is Creole, a dialect derived in part from French. Unfortunately, Creole is so different from French that it is unintelligible to those who speak French alone. Only recently has an alphabet been devised for Creole and little reading matter is available, a fact which helps explain the slow spread of literacy in Haiti.

Traces of the former French occupation are also seen in the locations of many of the towns on or near the coast. Although most of them were partly destroyed in the revolution, they did not cease to exist. Many of the smaller administrative subdivisions also date back to colonial days.

Relics of the revolutionary period itself are several fortresses built to prevent a French reconquest. Of these by far the most spectacular is the Citadelle Laferrière, a massive construction erected by the first Emperor of Haiti, Henri Christophe, as a final retreat in case of general defeat. A site was chosen upon the crest of a precipitous limestone ridge 2,600 feet high overlooking the Plaine du Nord. Here, with incredible labour, great ramparts ten feet thick were raised to heights of up to 130 feet. On human backs, hundreds of cannon and thousands of cannon balls were brought in along the steep rocky trail which was the only link between the hilltop and the plain below.

The fortress was never completed, nor was it ever needed to fulfil its intended function, but it still looms as the most ambitious human achievement in the Département. Now, from the village of Milot, four miles distant and the site of Christophe's ruined palace, tourists ascend to the Citadelle on horseback or on foot.

More recent events of geographic significance include the re-establishment, on a limited scale, of plantation agriculture on the northern plain. Sugar, however, has yielded the primacy to sisal, a tolerant crop which will grow in relatively poor land, not well suited to food production.

Another plantation crop is rubber. Many years ago a small grove of hevea trees was successfully planted in the Port Margot Valley, but no extension of rubber production was attempted until after the loss of southeastern Asia in the Second World War. After that disaster, a programme was set up by the United States government to attempt to develop a source of this commodity in the Département du Nord and elsewhere in Haiti. A large part of the Port Margot Valley was planted in hevea trees which have since come into production and are making a modest contribution to the exports of the country. To bring in an earlier yield, however, hope was placed on a quick-growing indigenous vine, known as cryptostegia, with a milky sap which contains a high proportion of latex. Large areas in and around the Limbé and Port Margot valleys were planted in cryptostegia, but this part of the programme resulted in complete failure. It was set in motion without adequate knowledge of local edaphic, biotic, or social conditions and was abandoned before any significant amounts of rubber had been produced. Unfortunately, though most of the land has reverted to food crops, it is now less productive than it was before the initiation of this experiment.

During and immediately after the last war, Haiti was also looked to as a source of bananas for the United States market. A number of plantations were set up in the northern plain and in addition the peasants were encouraged to grow bananas for export on their own holdings. For various reasons this activity also collapsed. Bananas now scarcely exist as a peasant crop, though a few plantations survive.

It is, perhaps, worth noting that the ease with which land has been acquired for commercial agriculture is closely related to the absence of any clear title to the land on the part of the peasant. The action of the government in supporting these acquisitions has not always been above reproach; the peasant has often received compensation only in the coin of bitterness and resentment.

One further influence of the past upon the present is found in the relations between Haiti and its eastern neighbour. As the population density in Haiti is considerably higher than that in the Dominican Republic, there has been much pressure on the international boundary. In some places the frontier has actually been shifted to the east, as is attested by the presence of many Spanish place names in central Haiti. The more common expression of this pressure, however, has been a steady, surreptitious migration of Haitians across the border in search of land and employment.

In 1937 the Dominican Republic undertook to exterminate or forcibly expel from its borders a large number of these illegal immigrants, and to assist in their repatriation the Haitian government set up various agricultural "colonies." Two of these lie within the Département du Nord in the northern plain, not far from the border. Also, in order to minimize friction, Haitians have been forbidden by their government to build their homes within one kilometre of the frontier in certain sections.

One instance of co-operation between the two countries was the construction, under the terms of the Treaty of 1929, of the Route Internationale, which forms the international frontier in the extreme southeast of the Département. Previously the border had followed the Libon River and was paralleled by no road on either side. This accord gave both countries a north-south route on the basis of shared construction and maintenance costs, the road itself belonging to neither state. Actually the benefits of this arrangement accrue mainly to the Dominican Republic. The Route Internationale is an integral part of the Dominican road network while its connection with main Haitian roads is devious and very little used. Since, moreover, the road was built about half a mile to the west of the Libon, Haiti lost a not inconsiderable strip of its national territory.

Administration

For administrative purposes, the Département is broken down into eight divisions, known as arrondissements. The smallest of these both in size and population is the Arrondissement of Limbé with 238 square kilometres and 39,593 people. The largest arrondissement is that of Vallière which has an area of 817 square kilometres, while the most heavily populated is that of Cap Haitien with 118,185 inhabitants.

The arrondissements are divided into a total of twenty-eight communes, the maximum number of communes per arrondissement being six, while the Arrondissement of Limbé consists of a single commune. This is the most populous of the communes, while the one with the lowest population is the Commune of Perches with only 3,746 people. Perches is also the smallest commune, having an area of 65 square kilometres, while the largest, the Commune of Fort Liberté, contains 271 square kilometres.

The communes are further subdivided into sections rurales, which are no more uniform in size than the communes and arrondissements.

Wherever possible, administrative boundaries follow physiographic features. Watersheds form the most common political divides, though in many places streams are used as well.

The Département as a whole is administered from Cap Haitien. In the extreme southeastern corner of the Département, however, military and health services are administered from Hinche, the leading town of the Central Plateau, but not itself a département capital.

Population

The population of the Département, according to the census of 1950,[4]

[4]The census of 1950 was the first general census to be undertaken in Haiti. Unfamiliarity with census procedures and objectives on the part of the native peasantry and even of the enumerators themselves made it impossible to achieve a high level of accuracy, and it is generally felt that the population figures recorded are too low. Estimates of the magnitude of the error range upwards to 30 per cent. Since, however, no other figures are available, and since relative densities are of greater significance than absolute densities, the values given in the census are used throughout this study.

was 539,049, or approximately 18 per cent of the total population of
Haiti. The average population density was thus 341 persons per square
mile. Nevertheless, as indicated in Figure 4, regional densities deviate

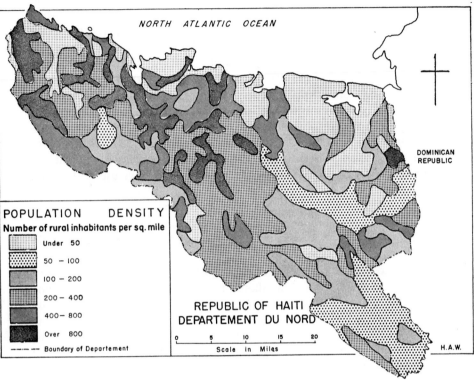

Figure 4. Population Density

markedly from this average figure. Much of the humid northwestern part
of the Département, particularly inland valleys and well-drained sections
of the coastal plain, contain over 800 persons per square mile. To the
east and south, densities are considerably lower but even here average
approximately 100 per square mile. Locally also the pattern of population density is characteristically uneven. Areas with very different
densities lie in close proximity one to another, and the zones of uniform
density are of limited extent.

Economy
Of the total population of the Département 464,953, or 86.3 per cent
are classed in the census as rural residents, while 74,096, or 13.7 per
cent are listed as urban. Of this last number, about one-third, or 24,229,
live in Cap Haitien, the leading city of the Département. Actually the

census takes a rather liberal view of what constitutes an "urban" community, for many of the "urban" centres listed contain only a few hundred people, most of whom depend directly on agriculture for their subsistence. Nevertheless, roughly the same ratio exists between followers of rural and urban occupations as between rural and urban dwellers. Agriculture, fishing and forestry employ 86 per cent of the total working population of 244,188. The corresponding figure for artisans, industrial workers and apprentices is 5 per cent; for those employed in commerce 4.1 per cent; for domestic servants 3.9 per cent, and for professional people and civil servants 1 per cent. Hence by far the greater proportion of the population of the Département lives directly from the land. Since, moreover, all industry is based on agricultural or forest products, and since these products and their derivatives form the sole exports from the Département, one may state that the entire economy of this area is founded on the productive use of the land.

About 7 per cent of the total area of the Département is in large plantations, all of which are located in the coastal lowlands. Sisal is grown mainly in the semi-arid east and rubber in the humid west, while sugar and bananas occupy an area intermediate in position and in precipitation effectiveness.

Over most of the remainder of the Département, sedentary subsistence agriculture is carried on. This should not be taken to suggest that some crops are not grown essentially for cash, or that crops grown normally for food are not exchanged commercially. Throughout the hills of the northwestern section of the Département, and in the adjacent plains, coffee is grown in small holdings, basically for export. Some cacao and tobacco are also produced for the same purpose. In addition, around the margins of the sisal and sugar plantations, many of the peasants devote some land to the production of these crops for sale to the companies concerned.

Intradepartmental trade in native food crops arises in part to supply the urban dwellers and in part because of local differences in the level and the seasonality of production, as indicated in Figure 5. It is noteworthy that the northeast sisal area and the extreme southeast never produce enough food to satisfy local requirements, while in the northwestern hills and in adjacent sections of the northern plain food is almost always available. People in the remainder of the Département experience both periods of surplus and periods of deficiency, but, fortunately, these are not everywhere of the same relative magnitude, nor do they occur everywhere at the same time. Hence, local famines may be largely prevented or mitigated by the exchange of food over relatively short distances.

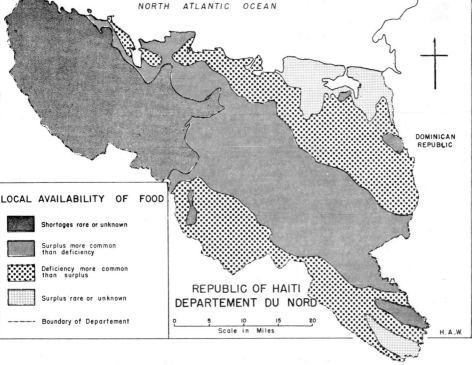

Figure 5. Local Availability of Food

Farming Techniques

The agricultural tools and methods of the Haitian peasant are similar to those used by subsistence farmers in most parts of the tropics. The machete and the hoe are almost the only implements used. Land is cleared by cutting and burning, and the crops are planted in small holes usually dug with the machete. Periodically weeds are removed, usually with the hoe. Harvesting is by hand.

Intensity of Land Use

The intensity of land use varies considerably, as may be seen in Figure 6. Throughout most of the southeastern, mountainous section of the Département, after each period of cultivation the fields are allowed to lie idle for three or four years or even longer, during which time a fairly dense cover of shrubs and small trees develops. At any one time only 30 to 50 per cent of the land is under crops. On the other hand, in the northwestern hills the land is seldom rested for more than two years at

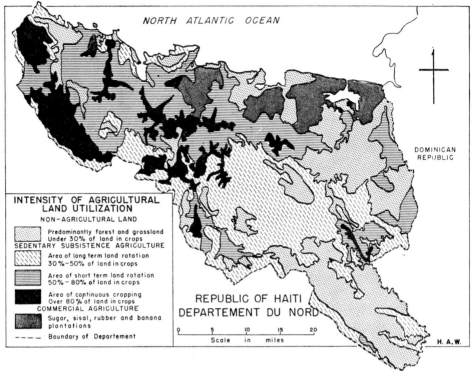

INTENSITY OF AGRICULTURAL
LAND UTILIZATION
NON-AGRICULTURAL LAND

Predominantly forest and grassland
Under 30% of land in crops

SEDENTARY SUBSISTENCE AGRICULTURE

Area of long term land rotation
30%-50% of land in crops

Area of short term land rotation
50% - 80% of land in crops

Area of continuous cropping
Over 80% of land in crops

COMMERCIAL AGRICULTURE

Sugar, sisal, rubber and banana
plantations

– – – – Boundary of Departement

NORTH ATLANTIC OCEAN

DOMINICAN REPUBLIC

REPUBLIC OF HAITI
DEPARTEMENT DU NORD

Scale   in   miles

0   5   10   15   20

H. A.W.

Figure 6.   Intensity of Agricultural Land Utilization

a time. Here, 50 to 80 per cent of the land is under cultivation at any
one time, and, of the remainder, a large part is used for grazing. Indeed,
in some broad valleys and on piedmont slopes facing the northern plain,
one finds areas where the land is cropped continually or where, if a rest
period is used, it is only seasonal.

Within the plain itself, in the subsistence farming areas, which lie
principally in the west, a short-term land rotation is practised. The land
is commonly withdrawn from cultivation but only for periods of one or
two years; some areas are replanted each rainy season.

On the Central Plateau, conditions are somewhat similar to those on
the plains, though continuous cropping is possible only under irrigation.

In addition, here and there throughout the Département, one finds
areas in which most of the land is in grasses or forest. These areas are
most extensive in the northeast and southeast. In them, agriculture
assumes a secondary position with respect to the land use pattern, but
not necessarily in the local economy. As a very broad generalization one

can say that, in the land mapped in Figure 6 as non-agricultural, grasses, xerophytic forest, and mangroves occupy areas of low relief whereas coniferous forest covers the hills. Some grazing is carried out in the grasslands and in both the coniferous and xerophytic forest. The coniferous forest is also used to some extent as a source of lumber, while firewood is taken from the mangroves.

Land Tenure

Large land holdings are found only in the various commercial plantations. Throughout most of the Département the system of small land holdings which developed after the Revolution has persisted and has indeed been accentuated by the practice, adapted from the French legal code, of dividing the property of a deceased person among all his legal heirs.[5] According to the 1950 census, the cultivated land available to each peasant household averages only 5.25 acres.

The census data also make it possible to estimate that, among households dependent on agriculture, the amount of cultivated land per capita is 1.215 acres. For small families, however, the figure is greater. Where there is but one member, cultivated acreage averages 3.93. Households of two persons have 2.15 acres per capita, those of three have 1.60, and those of four have 1.30.

With households of more than five persons, the amount of cultivated land per capita is below the departmental average. For establishments of five persons the figure is 1.13 acres, for those of six it is 1.06, and for those of seven it falls to 1.0. For still larger households, however, no further appreciable decline is registered. Even households of sixteen or more members have an average of 0.98 acres per person.

These departmental averages, of course, mask great regional differences, which arise from variations in the carrying capacity of the land, but which are merely hinted at in the census. Thus, 794 holdings each over sixteen acres in size are occupied by families of no more than three members; presumably these farms are located on relatively poor land. On the other hand, 630 households of ten or more persons have less than a single acre of cultivated land per household, while a further 1,168 households of similar size each subsist on farms between one and two acres in size. Land holdings with so many people per acre are undoubtedly located in the most productive sections of the Département and are probably also in places offering some paid employment, as, for example, on plantations.

[5]M. A. Holly, *Agriculture in Haiti* (New York, 1955), p. 45.

Land holdings are not only small but in many cases they are also fragmented. Only 28.2 per cent of the farms consist entirely of land around the farm home. In 48.8 per cent of all cases, other non-contiguous parcels are included in addition to the home plot, while 23 per cent of the farm units consist only of land, in single or multiple parcels, some distance from the residence of the farmer.

A result of this scattering of holdings is that a good deal of time is spent in travel to and from the fields. In most cases the journey is made on foot; if a horse, mule, or donkey is available, it is used normally to carry the crop, not the farmer. Nevertheless, the fragmentation has certain advantages, especially if the various plots are in areas which differ physically from one another to the extent that they produce different crops or the same crops at different times of the year. Under these conditions, most peasants consider a fragmentation of holdings to be definitely desirable.

According to the census, 83 per cent of the peasant families own the land they cultivate. Those who rent their land from the state number 2.5 per cent of the total, while 3.1 per cent rent their land from individuals. Paid managers are found on 4.6 per cent of the farms, and the remaining properties (4.8 per cent) are operated by sharecroppers, who, in lieu of a cash rent, turn over to the landowner one quarter to one half of the crop. Hired farm help, outside the plantations, does not account for more than four per cent of the total farm labour force.

Living Standards

By all material standards, the Haitian people are poor. Except in Cap Haitien, as noted below, and in some of the other towns, dwellings are made on a framework of roughly squared poles; they are walled with mud-daubed wattle, roofed with grass or palm thatch, floored with beaten earth or pebbles, and occasionally whitewashed. Approximate dimensions are from eight by fifteen to twelve by twenty feet, and the interior is commonly partitioned into two or three rooms. Water is obtained from the nearest stream or, in some cases, from a well, and 92 per cent of all dwellings, including those of Cap Haitien, have no sanitary facilities, even pit latrines.[6] Lighting is by small kerosene-burning lamps, locally made from tin cans. Cooking is done in a small booth outside the house.

House furnishings consist mainly of home-made tables and chairs, one or more cupboards, and one or two beds. In most households several members have no beds and sleep on mats on the floor. Pots, pans,

[6]Census of 1950.

dishes, and cups are mostly of cheap imported enamel-ware, and a few knives, forks, spoons, and glasses are usually to be found.

Another imported item is cloth for bedding and for clothing. Most people have one reasonably respectable outfit, including shoes, for special occasions. From day to day, however, they wear rather ragged apparel and prefer to go barefoot or shod in sandals made of old tires.

The food supply, as indicated above, varies considerably from place to place and from season to season, but people everywhere use in their diet such items as corn, rice, plantains, and various root crops including manioc, sweet potatoes, and taro. As well, a few vegetables and a number of wild greens are eaten. Occasionally a meal includes a chicken, some beef, pork, or goat meat, some Canadian salt cod, or, near the coast, some fresh fish.

As for the adequacy of this diet in terms of calories, vitamins, and minerals, no information is available, but undoubtedly most Haitians are undernourished. Even in areas mapped in Figure 5 as having no shortages, it is only the common vegetable foods which are always available, and even in these areas food prices may be so high that many needy folk must go hungry. Everywhere, too, the amount of food stored up for emergencies is low.

Without reliable sources of water, sanitary facilities, or an adequate diet, the people of Haiti are susceptible to many diseases. Despite the lack of reliable statistics, tuberculosis is believed to be the principal cause of death, and a great many persons suffer from yaws, malaria, or hookworm.[7] Life expectancy is 32 years at birth and reaches a maximum of 40 years at age five, by which time 30 per cent of all infants have died.[8] Only 6.5 per cent of the population is over 60 years of age.[9]

Nevertheless, most of the individuals one sees are of fine physique and appear robust. Certainly, the distance walked, the loads carried, and the manual labour expended in agriculture and other productive activities indicate that the Haitians possess considerable physical vigour.

It must be stressed that not everyone in the Département lives under the conditions described above. A few thousand merchants, civil servants, professional people, and skilled artisans are able to afford substantially better living quarters, good food, and such imported luxuries as watches, radios, bicycles, and even cars. Yet for the vast majority of the population, life offers little more than the elements essential for survival with a

[7]United Nations, *Mission to Haiti* (Lake Success, N.Y., 1949), pp. 60–75.
[8]*Bulletin trimestriel de statistique*, no. 21 (Port-au-Prince, June, 1956). Data are for all of Haiti.
[9]Census of 1960. Data for the Département du Nord.

minimum of comfort and without the possibility of any major cultural achievement.

Measured by ordinary yardsticks, then, the living standard of the Haitian peasant is one of the lowest in the Western Hemisphere, and unquestionably the lowest to be found in the Greater Antilles. Yet in their own evaluation of their situation the Haitians include also other values among which perhaps the most important are freedom from interference and from excessive economic competition one with another. In terms of these criteria, the farmers of Haiti live at a level which members of more affluent societies might well regard with envy.

Transportation and Trade

The major centre of foreign trade is the port of Cap Haitien, with docking facilities for ships drawing up to twenty-four feet. Direct overseas shipments also take place to and from sisal factories on the Bays of Caracol and Fort Liberté, goods being transferred from ship to shore by lighter. Small coastal towns to the west of Cap Haitien are connected with the larger port by schooners and tiny motor vessels.

There are only two good roads within the Département. The more important of these, the highway linking Cap Haitien with the Capital, Port-au-Prince, runs westwards, mainly along the plain, from Cap Haitien to Limbé, from which point it strikes south across the ridges of the Massif du Nord. The greater part of this road is paved.

A second paved road, with a paved sideroad to Milot, runs eastwards from Cap Haitien, through the northern plain. This highway terminates at the border town of Ounamenthe, from which point a secondary road leads into the Dominican Republic. Other secondary roads, usable throughout much, if not most of the year, reach all communities in the Département with populations exceeding five hundred. Some of the roads are suitable for passenger automobiles; others can only be used by trucks or jeeps. Only a few are well travelled; many see most of their activity on market-days, when they permit the passage of incoming trucks carrying passengers as well as a variety of freight, including cloth, soap, flour, bottled soft drinks, farm tools, and other manufactured articles. On their return journeys, the vehicles transport sacks of coffee, orange peel, or other products for export, as well as bags of rice, bunches of plantains, baskets of chickens, and other food for the urban markets.

In the main, however, the transportation of food to the cities as well as between rural districts is carried out on the backs of donkeys, horses, and mules or on the heads of women. In this, the most vital type of commercial movement, motor roads, though utilized, are not essential.

A network of paths links together all parts of the Département. Striking across the plains, twisting through valleys, snaking up mountain slopes, balanced on knife-edge ridges, run "grands chemins" often only a foot or two in width, and over them pass, on unshod feet, the animal and human carriers which provide the truly indispensable economic contacts. Such transportation, though primtive, is in most cases adequate. It might be considered inefficient if the women had alternative and more profitable ways of spending their time than in going to and from market, but most do not. In any case, an elimination of the present expenditure of time in travel and of land in the raising of pack animals would scarcely justify the high costs of road construction and maintenance, and of the purchase, repair, and fuelling of motor vehicles. Some road improvement and extension are desirable but northern Haiti, like most tropical areas, cannot economically support a dense network of good roads.

Population Mobility

At the present time the Haitian peasant seldom moves from one farm to another. This lack of mobility is not due to an ignorance of a possibly greater prosperity in areas other than that in which he lives, but in large part to the difficulty of obtaining land in these areas. Another factor discouraging his movement is religious, for the spirits he worships are closely associated with the land. The writer once asked two women living in what seemed to be a particularly desolate spot why they did not move. One woman muttered something which he did not catch, but to which the other made the sharp rejoinder, "The spirits would allow us to leave if it were a matter of life and death." Of the total population of the Département outside Cap Haitien, 92 per cent live within the communes in which they were born.

SUMMARY

In many respects, the Département du Nord of the Republic of Haiti is typical of areas of peasant agriculture throughout the humid tropics. Elsewhere in Latin America, as well as in Africa, Asia, and in the islands of the Pacific, millions of farmers similarly till small fields, scattered, apparently haphazardly, over hills as well as plains. The tools of the Haitian peasant and his means of transportation also differ little from those of hosts of other peasant farmers.

Nevertheless, Haiti differs from most other tropical areas in its history. Here, the effect of past events has been to suppress rather than to enhance local racial, social, and cultural variations. In few parts of the modern world will one find so homogeneous a culture and so classless a society as in rural Haiti.

Yet, despite the uniformity of the cultural environment, great contrasts exist in the patterns of land use. These contrasts arise in response to the Département's physical diversity: geologic, climatic, and edaphic. For this reason, and because of its high population density, northern Haiti provides an ideal setting for an examination of the adjustment of primitive people to physical conditions within a tropical setting.

2. Geology and Morphology

IN ANY GEOGRAPHIC AREA, the most important physical elements are structure and climate. These are relatively independent one of the other, and there is no hard and fast rule as to the order in which they should be presented. However, in places, like the Département du Nord, where much of the rainfall is orographic, an understanding of the climate requires a prior knowledge of the surface configuration. In turn, the character and disposition of surface features cannot be appreciated except through a consideration of their origins. Consequently, the exposition of the physical nature of the Département commences with an analysis of its landforms, discussed from a genetic point of view.

Rock Structure

The major geologic and physiographic divisions of the Département are shown in Figure 16, and a cross-section running roughly north and south through the western end of the Département is shown in Figure 7. Essentially the structure is that of an anticline with its axis extending in a northwest-southeast direction and plunging to the northwest. Some secondary folds and faults are also present.

Within the area of outcropping of this anticline may be found two of the three main physiographic subdivisions of the Département: the Massif du Nord and the Plaine du Nord. The third subdivision, comprising a small portion of the Central Plateau of Hispaniola, lies within a broad synclinorium to the southwest of the anticline.

The core of the anticline consists of granite and quartz diorite. This core was overlain, first by beds of shale, then by beds of limestone. Subsequently, between the basement rock and the overlying sediments

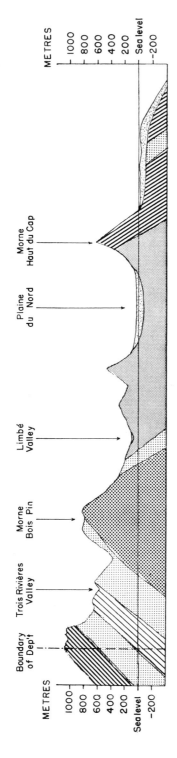

GEOLOGICAL CROSS SECTION

(FOR LOCATION SEE FIGURE 16)

Figure 7. Geological Cross-section

occurred extensive intrusions, first of basalt and later of andesite.[1] All the rocks composing the anticline are of Cretaceous or Eocene age.[2] Their characteristics are summarized in Appendix A.

Dissection

After its formation, the anticline was probably peneplaned, then uplifted and redissected. The accordance of eight peaks, distributed through the three major classes of rock, yet all between 3,450 and 3,800 feet high, suggests the presence of a former erosion surface. Nevertheless, level ground is now found only at lower elevations, and most of the upland is a maze of steep, narrow ridges and valleys.

The largest lowland lies on the northeastern flank of the anticline, where erosion has been effected both by waves and running water. These agents have largely removed the relatively soft basalts and shales which lie between the anticlinal core and the marginal ridge of massive limestone. In addition, east of Cap Haitien, the limestone itself has been worn away by waves to a level below that of the sea. Between Perches and Ounamenthe, marine activity has also carved a broad platform into quartz diorite and granite rocks.[3]

Within the Massif itself, erosion has been carried out exclusively by streams. The relation between rock type and landforms is therefore a close one. Granite and limestone outcroppings, resistant to erosion, form ridges, of which those of limestone are particularly lofty and continuous. In some places, ridges are also formed in quartz diorite, though this type of rock has more generally been eroded to form valleys of moderate breadth and depth. Shale is associated primarily with valleys; numerous shale hills exist, but most are relatively low. Areas of volcanic rock, like those of shale, are easily eroded and tend also to be rather low-lying. Nevertheless, two peaks formed by fairly recent effusion rise nearly as high as the summits of granite and limestone. One, about three miles west of the town of Plaisance, is Morne Mapoux, crowned with ash and still showing vestiges of a crater. The other, south of Carice, is also capped with deposits of ash and is aptly named Morne à Tuf.

Development of Intermontane Basins

During the early stages of the dissection of the anticline most of the drainage was either to the south or west (Figure 9). Probably only about one quarter of the Département drained directly northwards to the Atlantic. Because of the round-about routes taken by most of the streams on their way to the sea, their average gradients were low. And

[1]Woodring *et al.*, *Geology*, p. 267.
[2]Butterlin, *Géologie*, pp. 150–7.
[3]Woodring *et al.*, *Geology*, p. 357.

because they all had, in places, to pass from zones of soft rock through more resistant formations, many of them tended to acquire characteristics of maturity in sections of their upper courses. Several basins both large and small, were produced in this way.

In the northeast of the Massif, the Rivière Ténèbres and its tributaries carved, within a zone of quartz diorite rock, an extensive plain, here called the Carice Basin. Further downcutting was inhibited by the presence of a ridge of granite downstream, through which the river ran in a narrow gorge.

Eroded partly in quartz diorite and partly in shale was another broad flat-floored valley, extending from the latitude of the town of Grande Rivière south nearly to the boundary of the Département. This lowland is referred to here as the Ranquitte Basin; the obstruction prerequisite to its formation was the great limestone ridge which forms much of the southern border of the Département.

This same obstruction was also responsible for the development of two other plains, carved in shale, one at the southeast, the other at the northwest extremity of the Département. These plains have been named by the writer the Cerca la Source Basin and the Plaisance Basin, respectively, after their chief towns.

The same belt of limestone also contains several smaller valleys, flat-floored but relatively deep and narrow, and excavated, for the most part, in belts of shale occurring between beds of limestone. The largest of these valleys contains the town of Dondon, and is here identified by that name.

Middle and Late Tertiary Sedimentation

Much of the material eroded from the Massif was deposited, from Oligocene to Pliocene times, within the synclinorium to the south and on the wave-cut platform of the northeast. Evidently the run-off was very vigorous, for sediments remaining from this period are largely coarse-textured conglomerates, formed of well-rounded crystalline pebbles and boulders. Immediately to the south of the anticline, however, the material deposited was calcareous in nature. Here, beds of marl are found instead of, or in some places overlying, the conglomerate. Eventually most, if not all, of the Central Plateau was covered by alluvial silt and fine sand.

Stream Piracy

After the formation of the intermontane basins and the deposition of alluvium in the Central Plateau, there followed a period of stream rejuvenation caused in the main by a series of stream captures affecting the entire plateau area (Figures 8 and 9).

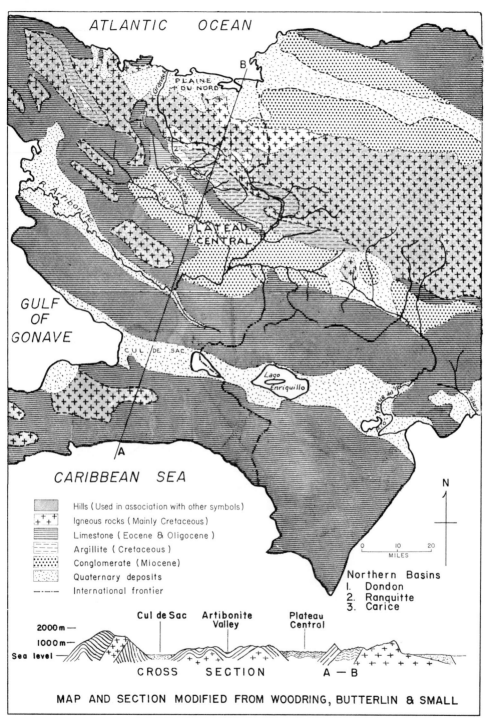

Figure 8.   Central Hispaniola, Geology and Relief

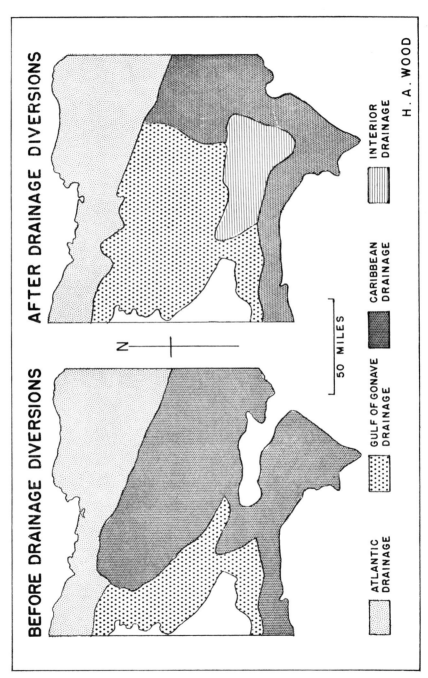

Figure 9. Central Hispaniola, Drainage Areas

BEFORE DRAINAGE DIVERSIONS

AFTER DRAINAGE DIVERSIONS

N

50 MILES

H. A. WOOD

ATLANTIC DRAINAGE

GULF OF GONAVE DRAINAGE

CARIBBEAN DRAINAGE

INTERIOR DRAINAGE

As a result of these drainage diversions, down-cutting was resumed throughout the Central Plateau, especially in the conglomerate area, where most of the land has been brought under slope, and where local relief is now of the order of 50 to 100 feet. On the other hand, in the areas underlain by limestone and marl there is little surface drainage and, though the main rivers have been quite deeply entrenched, the surface of the plain is still flat. The alluvial covering of silt and sand, has, nevertheless, been removed except on a few interfluves.

Evidence of renewed stream dissection may be seen not only in the Central Plateau but also in many southward draining valleys of the Massif. In both the Cerca la Source and Carice Basins, for example, most of the alluvium has been stripped away, and from one to three distinct terraces may be seen, the highest being about 45 feet above present river levels. On the other hand, no appreciable stream rejuvenation is evident in the Dondon Valley, which drains southward across a hard mass of limestone, and in the Plaisance Basin, which is drained to the north.

Other stream captures, of greater significance for the Département du Nord, have taken place across the northern ridges of the anticline, notably by the Grande Rivière.[4] This stream has captured the drainage from at least 200 square miles, including virtually the entire Ranquitte Basin, which formerly drained south towards the Central Plateau. In the area captured, downcutting has been so vigorous that the main streams are entrenched in huge gorges up to 500 feet in depth. Except around Ranquitte itself, only narrow scattered remnants of the old basin floor still exist, and nowhere can one find more than a few traces of the alluvium which formerly covered the valley floor. The Grande Rivière is still an active pirate stream and in time will extend its drainage area into the Central Plateau proper.

Minor instances of northward drainage diversions have occurred on the northern margin of the Carice Basin and at the extreme eastern end of the Plaisance Basin. The major parts of both basins have, however, not been affected.

Early Coastal Modifications

While streams were moulding the surface of the land, changes in coastline were being produced by wave action, alluviation, and coral building.

Along the eastern shore of the Département, partial protection was afforded by the peninsula of the Dominican Cordillera Septentrional. Hence, the waves, though created by the northeast trades, approached

[4]Wood, "Stream Piracy," p. 50.

the shore from various directions and were relatively feeble. A number of spits were built both eastwards and westwards but became prominent features only in places where conglomerates formed the shoreline and where, therefore, beach-building materials were abundant.

Farther west lay two major bays. The smaller of the two extended inland in an area now occupied in part by the valley of the Rivière du Trou. The larger bay occupied most of the western end of the present Plaine du Nord, being enclosed on the northwest by the Morne Haut du Cap, which at that time was an island. Within the bay itself, especially near its western end, were several smaller islands.

Into the mouths of both these bays, spits were constructed of debris derived from eroding basalt headlands. The smaller bay was partly enclosed by a four-mile spit, while the larger bay was almost completely cut off from the sea by a great bar, called by the writer the Limonade Bar after a town located near its southeastern extremity.

At the same time, offshore, a broad coral reef was developing on the eroded stumps of the limestone ridge which emerges from the sea farther west to form Morne Haut du Cap and other coastal hills. The reef, however, was not everywhere of the same breadth, nor was it unbroken. It was generally broader in the east than in the west, possibly reflecting differences in the breadth of its rock pedestal, and possibly also as an indirect result of the greater precipitation and run-off in the west. The reduced salinity and increased turbidity of coastal waters near stream outlets are conditions hostile to coral growth, as may readily be seen by the existence of gaps in the reef opposite the mouths of all major rivers in the area. Narrow gaps lay opposite the mouths of the Massacre, Marion, and Trou rivers, while the largest stream, the Grande Rivière, kept open a gap so broad as to constitute a major discontinuity in the reef.

Behind the reef, in the quiet waters of the lagoon, alluvial sediments now began to accumulate and great mangrove swamps developed.

Recent Coastal Modifications

The final modifications in the shoreline were initiated by an emergence of the coast east of the Grande Rivière and a submergence west of Cap Haitien. Near the Dominican border, the emergence was sufficient to raise the offshore reef above the sea. The reef now forms a broad rock plain with dimensions of approximately eleven miles by four, and a maximum elevation of some seventy feet above sea level. Behind the uplifted reef, two major lagoons remained, one on the international boundary, at the mouth of the Rivière Massacre, the other farther west at the mouth of the Marion. Channels through the main body of the reef provided both lagoons with direct outlets to the sea.

Of the two lagoons, the more easterly was originally the shallower, and receives the drainage of a large area. It has therefore been almost completely filled with alluvium. In contrast, the western lagoon still contains a stretch of open water measuring approximately 6½ miles from east to west by 1½ miles from north to south. The centre and the outlet of this lagoon are still over 10 fathoms deep. Known as Fort Liberté Bay, it is the finest harbour in the Département and, possibly, in all Haiti.

The western part of the zone of emergence was not uplifted sufficiently to produce any extensive coral plain. However, mangrove swamps were lifted above sea level to form poorly drained stretches of heavy clay. The clay was then partly covered by alluvium brought down by the two major rivers of the area, the Trou and the Grande.

These streams have also built cuspate deltas. That of the Trou is quite small, so small, indeed, that the water offshore, as a result of the scarcity of corals, is still quite deep. A small basin, known as Caracol Bay, still persists; its passage to the ocean through the outer lip of the reef is used by small ocean-going vessels, and is dredged to a depth of twenty-seven feet.

In contrast, the Grand Rivière, with a much larger drainage area, has a delta of considerable size, one which has been built seaward about four miles beyond the sand bar which formed the former shoreline in this area. Breakers from the open ocean pound upon the extremity of the delta, and have created a series of sand beaches extending both east and west.

Away from the two deltas, the water offshore is quite shallow and now supports a luxuriant growth of mangroves.

The Neutral Shore

Between the mouth of the Grande Rivière and the western limits of the Plaine du Nord no recent vertical movement has occurred, and the main characteristics of the coast reflect directly the actions of streams and waves. Of the two, the streams were the more important, for most of this area was a shallow lagoon, nearly cut off from the sea by islets, spits, and bars. From the humid highlands to the south many short streams flowed into the lagoon, filling it in almost completely. Of the resulting plain, much is still imperfectly drained, and some sections are still in swamp. The largest swamp is in the northeast, farthest from the source of sediment, yet reached by one small stream, the deposits of which have divided the swamp into two roughly equal parts. The upper part is fresh, while the lower section is tidal and largely filled with mangroves.

On the other hand, quite good drainage is characteristic of the eastern part of the plain, which contains extensive stretches of fine sand associated with the Grande Rivière delta, underlain, in places, by the gravels of the Limonade Bar.

The only example of wave activity which need be mentioned is the reworking of gravels of the Limonade Bar to produce a smaller, modern bar which forms the southeastern limit of Cap Haitien harbour. This bar provides a convenient connection between Cap Haitien and the plain to the east. Drainage from the south preserves a shallow gap at the northern end of the bar, and also maintains an opening through the main offshore reef, thus permitting shipping to enter the harbour.

The Submergent Shore

West of Cap Haitien the margin of the Massif du Nord has been submerged. A ridge of massive limestone parallels the coast, its scarp slope facing inland and its strata dipping steeply seawards. This ridge has been breached at four places, namely Acul Bay, the Limbé Valley, the Port Margot Valley and the Borgne Valley. The first three of these represent areas of extensive marine transgression, while the last-mentioned is of recent formation and is so narrow that little flooding has occurred.

On the seaward side of the massive limestone ridge are beds of a softer, impure limestone and of andesite. In many places these formations have been eroded away, but several remnants persist, of which those to the east were sufficiently separated from the main ridge to become islands when submergence occurred.

The submergent shore in its youthful state was thus extremely irregular. It has, however, been considerably straightened by streams and waves, particularly by the former. The Borgne and Port Margot valleys have been completely filled with alluvium, and that of the Limbé nearly so. Only Acul Bay, which receives no major river, is still essentially open. The action of waves has been to reduce in size the islands and promontories of soft rock, and, from the eroded materials, to build broad curving beaches in a great chain extending from Limbé Point to Baril du Boeuf Point. These strands pass a quarter to a half a mile seaward of the main limestone ridge; and behind the beaches, in areas not easily reached by sediments of the Port Margot and Limbé rivers, lagoons are still to be found. In most cases the water around the inner margins of the lagoons is fairly fresh, and instead of mangroves these areas have a natural vegetation of tall reeds.

West of Baril du Boeuf Point and east of Limbé Point, beaches are less in evidence since more of the shoreline in these areas is made up of the massive limestone, which contributes little beach-building material. Limbé Point itself, however, has been linked with the limestone ridge lying to the southeast by a narrow two-mile strand, formed largely from materials brought down by the Limbé River, which formerly entered the sea here.

Recent Colluvial Deposits
Through much of the Département the boundary between hills and plains is a sharp one. Many stretches of flat land were formed from alluvium brought down by a specific stream or streams and then carried out laterally to the foot of the hills. From the hills, especially where these were of limestone, little material was brought down on a broad front.

In lowlands surrounded by hills or slopes of basalt, however, conditions are quite different. Due to the low permeability and rapid erosion of the basalt, broad colluvial fans, composed mainly of angular gravels, have been built up along lower slopes in most of these areas. These fans are up to a mile wide in some sections of the emergent shore, and, due to partial drowning, are somewhat narrower in the submergent shore. Indeed, in the lower Port Margot and Limbé valleys, where the rate of alluviation is very high, fans can scarcely be detected. Another area of basalt hills without fans is in the extreme northeast, where, due to low precipitation, erosion is slow.

Recent Deposits of Coarse Alluvium
The most recent physical formations in the Département, and the last to be discussed, are gravel trains laid down in times of flood by streams descending from the highlands. All of these streams tend to flood their valleys whenever thunderstorms occur within their watersheds. The run-off is so rapid that a wall of water two or three feet high may often be seen rushing down the valley an hour or so after the rain has started. Vehicles have been known to start across a ford in relatively low water and be engulfed and carried away by the flood before reaching the other side. The storms usually strike in the early afternoon. Rivers rise before dark and reach their peak before midnight, but by morning the waters will have receded nearly to their pre-storm levels. Occasionally, as a result of the passage of a hurricane, longer flood periods will occur, but the sequence described above is more common and may take place several times a week during the rainy season.

The ribbons of rounded pebbles, gravel, and boulders laid down under these conditions are carried as far as the sea by only one stream, the Borgne. Elsewhere they terminate abruptly at those points upon the flood plain at which the carrying capacity of the streams drops below the critical value for gravel. Above and below these points the streams possess utterly different characteristics. Above, in the gravel trains, they are winding and braided and frequently change course in an unpredictable fashion. Below, flowing across the finer deposits of the alluvial plains, they march between well-defined banks, and though they may still meander, their changes in course are gradual, predictable, and in part controllable.

Although almost all streams have some stretches of gravel along their banks where they descend to the plains, gravel trains of mappable extent were found only on the six largest rivers of the north, the Borgne, Port Margot, Limbé, Grande, Trou and Massacre. In the first five the train is a long narrow strip following the river. That of the Massacre has a different shape, due to the fact that for most of its lower course that stream flows over an emerged plain into which it is incised. The gravel is not deposited until the stream reaches the low ground of the former lagoon north of Ounamenthe, and here it is laid down in a broad wedge-shaped fan.

SUMMARY

Upon a foundation of folded and slightly faulted rock of various types, the activity of running water and of waves has produced, in the Département du Nord, a great variety of landforms. The variety is the greater because this activity has been directed not against a static land mass, but against one which has been subjected to vertical movements differing locally not only in magnitude but in direction.

This complex geomorphic history is basically responsible for the intricacy of the patterns of soils, land use, and population density within the Département.

3. Climate

WHILE THE STRUCTURAL MORPHOLOGY of the Département produces an intricate pattern of geographical landscapes, the influence of climate gives rise to broader, but no less significant, regional differences. Because of the absence of weather stations in many sections of the Département, climatic boundaries cannot be drawn as precisely as physiographic ones. Nevertheless, the over-all picture is clear, and in many areas the precipitation records could be supplemented by information obtained through interviews.

Climatic Controls
The main climatic controls for the island of Hispaniola as a whole are more closely related to broad aspects of atmospheric circulation than to local conditions.

Most important is the prevailing atmospheric pressure. During the summer the area is dominated by the equatorial low and the summer low of the southern United States and Mexico, whereas during the winter atmospheric pressure rises under the influence of the North Atlantic high and the winter high of the southern United States and Mexico.[1] The average pressure difference from one season to the other is only 3 mm.,[2] but this is sufficient to bring about marked changes in other climatic elements.

For one thing, the pressure change causes a modification in the direction of the trade winds. During the winter, when pressure is relatively

[1]Alpert, "The Climate," p. 18.
[2]*Ibid.*

high and the isobars run east and west the winds blow strongly and steadily from the northeast towards the equatorial low. In summertime, the isobars assume a northwest-southeast orientation, and as winds are drawn in to the low pressure area of southern North America they cross Hispaniola from the southeast.[3]

The change in air pressure also results in a change in the stability of the air. During the summer period of low pressure, the air is relatively unstable, and thunderstorms are frequent. During the winter, with higher pressure and greater stability, thunderstorms rarely occur.[4]

Also related to the general circulation of the atmosphere is the passage of weak polar fronts during the winter. As large winter cyclones pass out into the Atlantic from the southeastern United States, polar continental air, swinging in from the northwest may travel sufficiently far to affect the northern coast of Haiti. The weather which develops is known as a "norther."[5] Northers reach a maximum in February, but may occur two or three times during any winter month. They do not bring heavy rain, but rather a prolonged light drizzle.

Finally, broad atmospheric conditions produce the tropical hurricanes that periodically visit the island. Since these storms usually cross the island before striking the Département du Nord, their presence here is felt less in terms of destructive winds than in torrential rains. The records of Tannehill[6] show that during the period 1900–1944 a total of thirty-five hurricanes passed close enough to the Département to produce rain. Of these four came in July, six in August, fourteen in September, six in October, and five in November. It should be noted that hurricanes occurring early in the season develop in the eastern Atlantic. If they strike the Département du Nord, they must first cross the entire island from east-south-east to west-north-west, losing much of their violence in so doing. In contrast, late-season storms tend to originate in the western Caribbean and then to travel north and northeast. They may thus reach the Département after crossing only a narrow strip of land, and their winds move more nearly at right angles to the shore. Consequently, particularly heavy rains commonly occur late in the hurricane season.[7]

The only local condition appreciably affecting climate is relief. Average temperatures, which are from 77° to 78°F. on the Plaine du Nord, drop, on the hills, by about 1°F. for each 330 feet of altitude.[8] The

---

[3]*Ibid.*, p. 20.
[4]*Ibid.*, p. 19.
[5]*Ibid.*, p. 24.
[6]I. R. Tannehill, *Hurricanes* (Princeton, 1945), pp. 163–238.
[7]For climatic statistics, see tables in Appendix B.
[8]Alpert, "Climate," p. 33.

location of major ridges is, of course, also a factor in the distribution of relief rain and the location of rain-shadow areas.

The Yearly Round of Weather in the Département du Nord

The weather year will be taken as beginning in May, this being the month of greatest uniformity of precipitation throughout the Département and of the slowest change in weather conditions.

In May, unstable air covers the Département, and the trade winds, coming from the southeast, blow offshore, though feebly and fitfully. Orographic rain is thus at a minimum but precipitation comes from convection showers. These affect all parts of the Département; the lowest average rainfall recorded for this month at any station is 4.8 inches, while values of 6 to 9 inches are more common. Since most of the thunderstorms originate in overheated inland valleys, the total amount of precipitation is somewhat higher in these locations than along the coast or on the Central Plateau, but all places are amply watered. Most areas receive rain on the average every three or four days. Temperatures on the coast average about 78°, with a mean minimum of 71° and a mean maximum of 85°.

In June the southeasterly trades have become more firmly established. Though the air is still unstable, its more vigorous lateral movement results in a reduced frequency of thunderstorms. These still occur, but all stations experience a decline in rainfall from the values recorded in May. In the mountains and on the plateau the decline is slight, but along the coast it is more pronounced, for the north-moving air, descending from the hills, is adiabatically heated and consequently made relatively dry. The only coastal area receiving nearly as much rain in June as in May is the northeastern part of the Plaine du Nord. This area is on the outer margin of the broadest part of the plain and evidently far enough from the mountains for the air to regain its instability. Elsewhere along the coast the amount of rain drops to 3 or 4 inches, about 60 per cent of the values for May. Temperatures are about two degrees higher than in that month, and very oppressive conditions prevail.

The trend observable between May and June continues on into July. Precipitation values continue to decline, though some thunderstorms still develop within the deeper valleys of the Massif. These storms bring 4 to 5 inches of rain to the hills and to some adjacent sections of the Plaine du Nord. On the other hand, over most of the plain, thunderstorms are rare, and precipitation is less than 2 inches. The extreme northeast, which receives 5 to 6 inches of rain in June, has less than an inch in July. Temperatures are generally slightly higher in July than in

June, but the difference is less than 1°F. Every ten years or so there may be a hurricane in July, but these storms have evidently no marked effect on precipitation averages.

In August the influence of hurricanes becomes noticeable. Though the greater proportion of rainfall still comes from thunderstorms, the amount contributed by hurricanes raises average precipitation figures above the values for July. The increase is not large, from half an inch to an inch at most stations, but it is fairly general. Since, however, hurricanes come on the average during only one August out of seven, in most years August precipitation is no greater than that of July. Temperatures are about the same.

September sees the peak of the hurricane season and also an increase in thunderstorm activity. The trades still blow from the southeast, but, as the pressure gradient is reduced, they blow less strongly than before, and convection currents are more readily established. Consequently there is a marked increase in precipitation. Coastal and northern plain stations experience an increase of 1½″ or 2″, to values of 4″ or 5″. In the mountains the increase is somewhat smaller, but sufficient to bring the monthly rainfall totals to 7″ to 10″ in the northwest, while even the south, despite its interior location, receives 5″ or 6″. September temperatures average about 80° on the coast, roughly the same as those of August.

The main changes in October are that hurricanes are fewer, and that sometime during this month the trade winds swing from the southeast to the northeast. The air is still relatively unstable, and during the period of light and uncertain wind direction there is an increase in the frequency of thunderstorms. This increase is sufficient to maintain, or slightly to increase, the total amount of rainfall at most stations, despite the decrease in hurricane precipitation.

Along the coast, however, another influence begins to be felt in October. For that part of the month in which the trade winds blow from the northeast, orographic rain occurs on the hills at the western end of the Département; Cap Haitien, Le Borgne, and Bayeux all register over 8″ for October. The area to the east, lying under the rain-shadow of the Cordillera Septentrional of the Dominican Republic, receives no significant quantities of relief rain, but, as indicated above, is fairly adequately watered by thunderstorms. October temperatures are similar to those in November.

By November the northeast trades are well established; air flows continuously across the island, and atmospheric pressure is rising. Consequently thunderstorm activity is sharply reduced and precipitation is fairly closely correlated with exposure. Stations on windward slopes of the northwestern hills receive upwards of 10″ of rain and even some intermontane valleys, not too far inland, receive nearly as much. The Central Plateau, in the rain-shadow of the Massif, is quite dry, with only about 2″ of rainfall. Also in a rain-shadow is the northeastern part of the coastal plain. This area, however, is on the average more rainy in November than in October due to the periodic heavy rains brought by November hurricanes. With the resumption of more or less constant northerly winds in November, temperatures in the Départe-ment at last decline from their summer levels. There is a general drop of 2° or 3°.

In December the hurricanes are over, the air is becoming more stable, and most of the precipitation is orographic or else produced by the few thunderstorms which still occur. All rainshadow areas are dry. Northeast parts of the Plaine du Nord receive under 2″ of rain, while less than one inch falls in the Central Plateau. However, north-facing slopes and adjacent lowlands still experience 4″ to 8″ of rain. Temperatures in December are 2° or 3° lower than the values for November. They average 74° to 76° along the coast with mean minima of about 67° and mean maxima of 80°.

By January, thunderstorms have almost ceased to develop, and, for most of the Département, the dry season is fully established. The trade winds still bring rain, however, to the seaward margin of the Massif, particularly in its western section. Here over 4″ of rain falls during the month, though the amount of precipitation declines sharply inland. In the Plaisance Valley, for example, January is the driest month of the year, with less than 3″ of rain. The rainfall in the Central Plateau and in the northeastern part of the Plaine du Nord is even lower than in December. A few northers may occur but they do not bring much rain. Temperatures are 1° or 2° lower than in the previous month.

February sees two main changes, a lessening of the persistence of the northeast trade winds and the maximum development of northers. The result is a slight redistribution of precipitation along the coast. The northers bring protracted but gentle showers to a fairly wide coastal zone, resulting in a slight increase in precipitation in some of the intermontane basins and in an area northeast of a line joining Le Trou and Cap Haitien. Northers also give rain to north-facing slopes in the western part of the Département, but not enough to offset a decline in the amount of precipitation brought by the trade winds. Hence this area, though still well-watered, suffers a slight reduction in precipita-tion. As the effect of the northers is limited to the coastal area, inland sections of the Département remain dry in February. The average temperature for February along the coast is about 73°, the lowest monthly mean for the year. Absolute minima of 57° have been recorded on the coast during the passage of northers and Dondon, in an intermontane valley not far inland, once recorded a low of 41°.[9]

In March, winter changes abruptly to summer. The trade winds shift from the northeast to the southeast, wind velocity declines, atmospheric pressure falls, and thunderstorms begin again. For most of the Département the total amount of precipitation is not high, ranging from 2″ to 3″. The northwestern hills, however, still have enough orographic rain to raise the monthly figures to 4″ or 5″. The change of seasons is seen in the temperatures as well as in the rainfall. Average temperatures rise by 1° or 2° on the coast and more sharply inland. Indeed the highest average absolute maximum temperatures for any month at Cap Haitien (92°) and Bayeux (95°) are those for March.

By April the summer pattern is all but fully established. In most years the northeast trades have ceased, and, with them, virtually all of the orographic rain in the Département. Atmospheric pressure is still dropping, and, as the air becomes increasingly unstable, thunderstorm activity is building up to its May maximum. Convection showers fall in all sections of the Département. Only one station records less than 3″ of rain while over half report 4″ or more. Average temperatures on the coast stand at about 77°, some 2° higher than in March and only 1° less than the figure for May.

Climatic Classification

The classification of tropical climates is one of the most difficult tasks confronting climatologists. The difficulties are due in part to the fact that most climatologists are less familiar with tropical than with temperate climates, and in part to the character of tropical precipitation. Much tropical rain comes in violent downpours, which give rise to heavy run-off, but make comparatively small additions to the ground water supply. Tropical precipitation totals cannot therefore be correlated precisely with the rate of soil moisture recharge. Rates of evaporation and transpiration in the tropics, also differ markedly from values obtaining in temperate areas. Furthermore, because of local edaphic and vegetational differences, the effectiveness of a single shower may vary greatly from place to place.

Consequently, in the tropics, climatic generalizations are often misleading. Any precise numerical values attributed to evaporation rates

---

[9]Alpert, "Climate," p. 41.

and to the amount of water stored in the soil are likely to be more impressive than realistic. Climatic classifications based on such values may correctly describe conditions in a few places, but they will not be generally valid.

For this reason the writer has adopted the very simple approach to the classification of tropical climates proposed by Mohr and Van Baren.[10] This classification is based entirely on monthly precipitation figures, and while it is recognized that these do not tell the whole story, the other major climatic variable, temperature, varies within such narrow limits in the Département that no major errors can result from treating it as constant. At least, it has been possible to avoid the construction of an elaborate classification upon a foundation of other values of assumed or questionable accuracy.

The system of Mohr and Van Baren makes only two major distinctions. Months with under 60 mm. (2.37″) of rain are classed as dry, whereas months with over 100mm. (3.94″) are considered wet. Months with intermediate amounts of rain are referred to as moist. The validity of these values has been supported by field studies carried out by several investigators.[11]

For each station the number of wet months is counted and then the number of dry months. A month with under 60 mm. of rain will not, however, be counted as dry if it follows immediately after a wet month, as in this case sufficient moisture will remain in the soil to delay the time at which the dry season really takes effect. The two figures are then written down one after the other, the number of wet months being placed first.[12] These figures indicate basically the duration of the rainy season and the duration of the dry season, those aspects of tropical climate which are of paramount importance from the point of view of agriculture and soil development. Mathematically, under this system, there could be as many as sixty-five separate climatic types, but in any one area only a fraction of these will exist, and the numbers can be reduced still further by a judicious grouping. Within the Département du Nord the number of classes recognized is seven.

This system works best where there is one main rainy season followed by one main dry season. This is, in fact, the situation prevailing in the Département du Nord although most stations record two precipitation maxima during the rainy season.

[10]E. C. J. Mohr, and F. A. Van Baren, *Tropical Soils* (The Hague, 1954), pp. 70–1.
[11]*Ibid.*, p. 69.
[12]Thus the notation (7 - 3) indicates a station with seven wet months, three dry months and, by subtraction, two moist months.

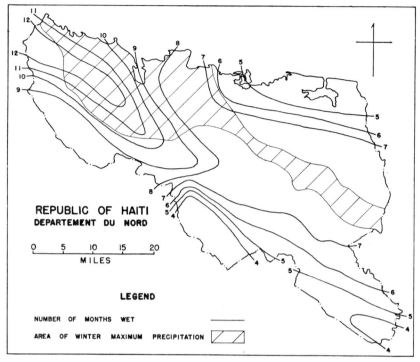

Figure 10.   Number of Months Wet

Climatic Types in the Département du Nord

The distribution of wet and dry months and of climatic types within the Département is shown in Figures 10 to 12. These maps also indicate the section of the Département which receives its maximum precipitation in winter, not in summer. Columnar rainfall diagrams for a representative station in each climatic type area are given in Figure 13.

TYPE I.   Here no really dry season occurs, though there is a period of relatively low rainfall. No months are classed as dry, and nine to twelve months in the year are wet. Climate of this type is found in the northwestern highlands of the Département, which receive summer convectional showers, autumn hurricanes, and winter orographic and frontal rain.

TYPE II.   This type is only slightly less humid than Type I. The wet season may be a bit shorter (8 - 0), or there may be a short dry period (9 - 1), falling in the winter in the south and in the summer in the north. Areas with Type II climate are peripheral to the more humid Type I zone.

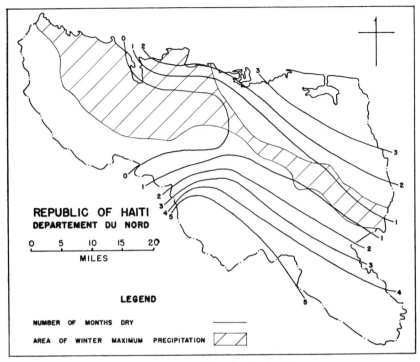

Figure 11.   Number of Months Dry

TYPE III.   Here the dry period is similar to that in the Type II climate, being at most one month in length, but the wet season is shorter, with a duration of only six to seven months. Areas with Type III climate lie at lower elevations or slightly to the east of the areas with Types I and II climates, but still within the zone which experiences winter orographic as well as summer convectional rain.

TYPE IV.   This climatic type covers a greater area than any other in the Département. It includes most of the southern highlands as well as the southeastern part of the Plaine du Nord. There is a well-defined dry season, occurring, in most sections, in the winter, but only two or three months long, indicating that the convectional precipitation is supplemented by orographic and frontal rain. On the northern slopes of the Massif, indeed, the greater part of the precipitation is of these latter types and the dry season comes in summer, when the north-moving air is adiabatically heated and dried. The rainy season in the Type IV climate, like that in the Type III climate, is six to seven months in duration.

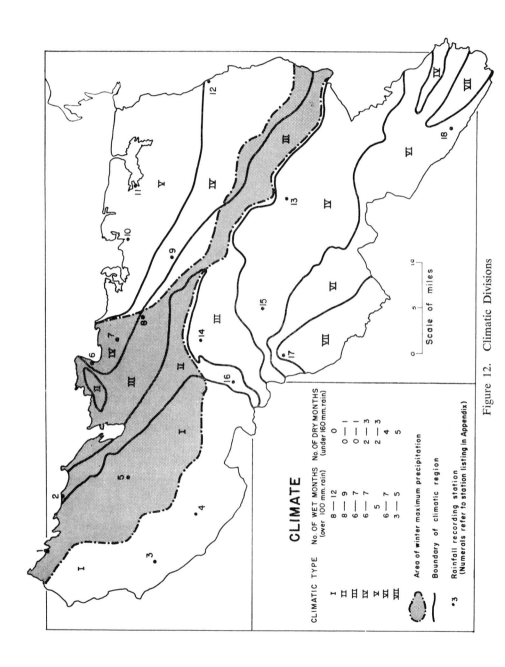

CLIMATE

CLIMATIC TYPE	No. OF WET MONTHS (over 100 mm. rain)	No. OF DRY MONTHS (under 160 mm. rain)
I	8 — 12	0
II	8 — 9	0 — 1
III	6 — 7	0 — 1
IV	6 — 7	2 — 3
V	5	2 — 3
VI	6 — 7	4
VII	3 — 5	5

Area of winter maximum precipitation

Boundary of climatic region

•3 Rainfall recording station.
(Numerals refer to station listing in Appendix)

Scale of miles

Figure 12. Climatic Divisions

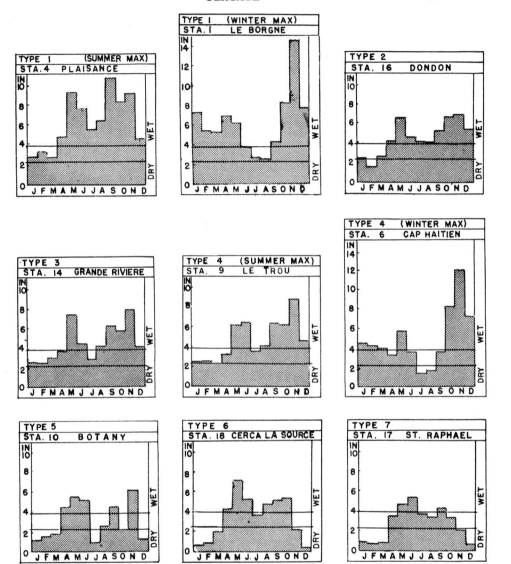

RAINFALL GRAPHS

FOR STATIONS OF EACH CLIMATIC TYPE

Figure 13. Climatic Graphs

TYPE V.   Only the northeastern part of the Plaine du Nord falls within this category. Here the wet period is considerably shorter than in the Type IV climate, being only five months in length, since this area does not receive relief rain. Nevertheless, due to the precipitation received from November hurricanes, the dry season, which comes in winter, is no longer than in Type IV climates.

TYPE VI.   Areas with this climatic type lie along the southern margin of the Massif and on the inland limit of Atlantic precipitation. Here the basins and valleys provide suitable sites for the development of early and late season thunderstorms, and their rains, together with some hurricane precipitation, cause the wet season to last six to seven months. The dry season, however, is acute, enduring for four months in the winter.

TYPE VII.   In this true interior climate, precipitation is derived almost entirely from summer thunderstorms. Only three or four months of the year are classed as wet while the dry season is five months in length. Two parts of the Département contain this type of climate; one is at the southeastern corner of the Cerca la Source Basin, the other lies within the Central Plateau.

Climatic Variability

Although the above outline is based on average precipitation and temperature values, it must be stressed that in many years conditions depart radically from the average. Extended droughts are not uncommon, particularly in the plains and eastern hills. Even Cap Haitien has experienced rainless periods of up to eleven months. Extended periods with above normal rainfall are also not uncommon; at Cap Haitien rain has been so continuous that public prayers have been held for its cessation.[13]

SUMMARY

Within the Département du Nord, some sections are continuously humid while others have so little rain that the land can be cultivated during only a few months each year. However, before one may most profitably examine the relation between the rainfall regime and the growth of crops, it is necessary to discuss the soils of the Département, for in their development climate also exercises a real, if indirect, influence on agriculture.

[13]Alpert, "Climate," p. 79.

4. Soils

Soils Classification

In classifying the soils of the Département a genetic approach has been taken, for two main reasons. First, such an approach is of the greatest geographical significance. With its emphasis on the part played in soil differentiation by parent material and climate, a genetic soils classification provides a major link between these elements of the physical environment on the one hand and the use of the land on the other. Secondly, it was discovered that only with such a classification was it possible to locate soils boundaries on aerial photographs of the scale available.

Such an approach does not, in fact, produce results which are fundamentally different from those which arise from a classification in terms of profile characteristics, and there is the added advantage that genetic soils classifications made in different parts of the world are more readily comparable with one another than classifications of other types.[1] A soils maps of the Département is presented as Figure 17.

[1]In Appendix C, soil types recognized by the writer in Haiti are compared with those identified in Puerto Rico by R. C. Roberts (*Soil Survey of Puerto Rico*, USDA Bur. Plant Ind. Ser. 1936, no. 8, 1942). Climatic and geologic conditions are somewhat similar in the two areas, and, although the classification of Roberts is not strictly genetic, it has been possible to associate one or more of his soil types with many, though not all, of the types identified in the Département. This association is helpful since data on crop yields, not available for Haiti, were obtained in Puerto Rico. Productivity ratings established for Puerto Rican soils should give a reasonable approximation of the agricultural value of similar soils in Haiti. These productivity ratings are given in Appendix D, a tabulation showing average yields, in percentages of a stated optimum, for

RESIDUAL SOILS

Gs.   *Shallow soil on granite*

This soil has developed through the weathering of granite bedrock on mountain slopes and on dissected granitic inliers in the Plaine du Nord. It occurs within climatic Types III and IV, areas with a wet season of six or seven months and a dry period of one to three months duration. Natural vegetation[2] is mainly pine forest, with or without stretches of open grassland. On the plains there is some mixed scrub and xerophytic forest. Slopes range generally from 20 per cent to 50 per cent.

Essentially this is a well-drained, friable quartz sand or sandy gravel, mixed with a certain proportion of clay derived from the breakdown of orthoclase in the rock. In depth, the overburden is less than 36 inches, and usually between 12 and 18 inches.[3]

The only evidences of profile development are a slight darkening of the surface layer and some preferential vertical movement of iron. Phosphorus and potassium are in short supply[4] and moisture-holding capacity is low. This soil is therefore of little value agriculturally, though in some areas certain tree crops can be grown.

GH.   *Granitic sand with hardpan*

This soil has developed from the Gs type in areas of level terrain and imperfect drainage with a pronounced dry season. Vegetation consists of grasses a foot or so in height.

The fluctuation of the water table together with the alternating upward and downward movement of soil solutions have resulted in the formation of an iron hardpan 6 to 24 inches below the surface. Above the hardpan

---

various crops in each soil. For the summary statements in the present chapter, percentages under 25 are considered very low, those from 25 to 50 as low, those from 50 to 75 as moderate, those from 75 to 100 as high, and those over 100 as very high.

[2]The author uses the term "natural vegetation" in this chapter not to refer to the original vegetation but to indicate the type of vegetation found at present in uncultivated areas.

[3]These values are somewhat greater than those found in other, more easily eroded types of rocks. In granite areas, the quartz particles hamper the lateral flow of soil solutions and promote relatively deep weathering (Mohr and Van Baren, *Tropical Soils*, p. 168).

[4]Use is made of the numerical criteria recognized as significant by the Haitian Department of Agriculture in determining the adequacy of the supply of these chemicals, viz: a soil of moderate fertility must contain 8 p.p.m. of assimilable nitrates, 75 lbs./acre of phosphorus and 100 lbs./acre of potassium.

the soil is an acid, homogeneous, medium-coarse, orange-brown sand. Fertility is extremely low; the hardpan impedes drainage and root penetration. Consequently this soil is almost useless for cultivation. Even the grasses provide little nourishment for livestock.

GM. *Mature granitic soil*

This soil has developed as a result of the prolonged weathering of granitic materials in areas of low relief and a Type IV climate. It is always found on level undissected land, in association with GH soils. GM soil occupies the higher central sections of the interfluves while GH soil is found in marginal locations. Natural vegetation is grasses with scattered xerophytic and mesophytic trees.

The profile consists of an A horizon of 10 inches of dark brown loam overlying a B horizon 4 to 12 inches deep of reddish-brown silty clay and a parent material of yellow-orange silty clay. Throughout the profile there is an abundance of angular, coarse quartz crystals. Drainage is moderate; plant foods, except nitrates, are reasonably plentiful; for most crops, yields are moderate.

Qw. *Youthful, well-drained quartz diorite soil*

This soil is formed by the weathering of quartz diorite in areas of hilly to rolling relief under climatic conditions ranging from those of Type I to Type IV. Vegetation is mainly deciduous forest though there are some xerophytic and coniferous stands as well.

The profile is no deeper than in the case of the youthful granitic soils, but the materials are of a finer texture reflecting the high proportion of rapidly disintegrating andesine in the quartz diorite. The overburden is usually 12 to 36 inches in depth, and drainage is moderate to good.

The A horizon consists of silt loam or silty clay, dark brown in colour and 6 to 15 inches deep, overlying a 6- to 24-inch B horizon similar in texture to the surface soil but red-brown in colour. There may also be a C horizon of yellow-orange clay loam, but in most cases the B horizon rests directly on the bedrock. Throughout the profile large quantities of coarse quartz crystals are intermingled with the finer materials. On most of the steepest slopes the A horizon has been eroded away.

Chemically the soil is slightly acid and of moderate fertility. It is particularly well suited to relatively tolerant crops such as rice, cotton, and tobacco.

QI. *Imperfectly drained quartz diorite soil*
Soil of this type has developed on quartz diorite in areas with similar climate and vegetation but with lower relief than the areas with Qw soils. The depth of the overburden generally exceeds 36 inches and drainage is moderate to imperfect.

The profile shows a 5- to 15-inch A horizon of dark brown to black loam over a 10-inch B horizon of reddish-orange silty clay and a C horizon of yellow-grey silty clay. Throughout the entire profile, coarse quartz grains are found in abundance.

The soil is slightly acid in reaction, of good moisture-holding capacity, but somewhat less fertile than the Qw soil due to a lower nitrogen content. Agriculturally it is quite useful, especially in areas which experience a long dry season.

QP. *Poorly drained quartz diorite soil*
This soil has developed on quartz diorite in level, poorly drained areas with a Type III climate and a vegetation of tall grasses and reeds. A layer of black muck 6 to 16 inches in depth overlies infertile yellow-and-orange mottled silty clay. Some grazing is carried on, but this soil is not used for growing crops.

QL. *Red lateritic soil on quartz diorite*
Soil of this type has developed on quartz diorite under broadleaf and coniferous forest in humid well-drained areas. Strong leaching with a continuous downward movement of soil solutions is essential for the formation of these soils, and they may be found on steep slopes in areas of high precipitation nearly all year (Climatic Types I and II) or else on gentle slopes in areas with moderate precipitation but little or no dry season (Type III).

The overburden often exceeds 12 to 15 feet in depth, and only on one occasion and at a depth of 4 feet was bedrock observed. In most places the A^1 horizon has been eroded away, but here and there it remains as a layer of medium dark brown clay loam up to 6 inches thick, and quite rich in organic matter. The A^2 horizon is a stone-free sandy loam, brick-red to a depth of 2 to 3 feet, and then becoming orange-red. The B horizon, containing white patches of kaolinite, is reached at depths of 9 to 15 feet.

Although its moisture-holding capacity is high, this soil has been leached of most of its phosphorus and potassium, and it is therefore of low fertility.

QYL. *Youthful lateritic soil on quartz diorite*
This soil has developed on quartz diorite in areas of low relief, slightly less humid and less well drained than areas with QL soil, but with similar vegetation.

The overburden is much shallower than in the QL soil, being four to eight feet in depth, and drainage is moderate.

In most places the A horizon has not been eroded away; it consists of a 6- to 18-inch layer of dark brown loam. The B horizon generally exceeds 18 inches in depth and is an orange-brown silty clay containing some white patches of kaolinite. The parent material, where observed, was an orange-white loam. Where the overburden is under 48 inches in depth some quartz crystals appear in the upper soil horizons, otherwise the profile is free from grit and stones. Chemically, this soil is similar to the QL soil, but the fertility is somewhat higher since less leaching has occurred.

VY. *Youthful soil on andesite*
This soil has developed on andesitic volcanic rock in areas of high relief and little or no dry season (Climatic Types I, II and III). Vegetation is broadleaf mesophytic forest.

In these areas the decomposition of the bedrock is very rapid.[5] Indeed, it is difficult to ascertain the exact depth of the regolith, for the upper layers of the bedrock are easily dug into with a shovel. Generally, however, it may be stated that the overburden is 4 to 5 feet in depth, except on cultivated slopes with gradients in excess of 70 per cent, where it may be no more than a foot deep. Even the steepest slopes have no rock outcrops.

The normal profile contains an A horizon of dark brown stone-free loam up to 12 inches thick over a B horizon of brown or grey-brown silt loam 5 to 15 inches deep. The parent material is an orange-brown silt loam with or without a little angular gravel. On the steepest slopes the C horizon is missing and the B lies directly upon the disintegrating bedrock. Drainage is moderate to imperfect. Because leaching is not far advanced, and because soluble salts are continually being released from the disintegrating bedrock, this soil is of relatively high fertility.

VL. *Lateritic soil on andesite*
This soil has developed on andesitic rock in humid well-drained areas.

---

[5]The labradorite and anorthite, which comprise much of the andesite, have a particularly high rate of weathering (Mohr and Van Baren, *Tropical Soils*, p. 114).

Like the lateritic quartz diorite soils, the VL soil type may be found on all slopes in areas of heavy rains in nearly all months (Climatic Types I and II). It also occurs on gentle slopes in areas with a shorter wet period, but little or no dry season (Type III).

This is a deep soil, reaching a depth of 10 feet or more. In fact, in areas with this soil, bedrock was never directly observed. The A horizon consists of a layer of red-brown silt loam up to 24 inches in depth over a B horizon of red silty clay which may turn orange at depths of 36 inches or more. Drainage is moderate to good and the entire profile is free from grit and stone. In many areas the A horizon has been removed by erosion.

Slightly acid, and with a good moisture-holding capacity, this soil is generally less fertile than VY soil, and is particularly low in phosphorus. Nevertheless, certain crops such as coffee, bananas, and citrus fruit can be grown with moderate success.

BY.   *Youthful soil on basalt*

This soil is found in areas with moderate to steep slopes (20 to 100 per cent) and under a variety of climatic conditions, ranging from those of Climatic Type I to those of Climatic Type V. Natural vegetation is broadleaf semi-deciduous or xerophytic forest.

The main mineral constituents of the basalt: augite and labradorite, have rates of weathering which are medium and very high, respectively.[6] Consequently the basalt breaks down very rapidly. The decomposition is also relatively complete since the basalt contains little material which resists weathering. There is no deep zone of disintegrating rock, comparable to that found in the andesite, in which the more quickly weathered minerals have already broken down, but more resistant ones remain to form separate, loose granules. Instead the transition between consolidated and unconsolidated material is accomplished in a fairly shallow zone. As a result, the downward movement in basalt of soil solutions is less free than in andesite or, indeed, in granite or quartz diorite.

Since, therefore, almost all of the moisture derived from precipitation must escape laterally, the rate of erosion in basalt soils is higher than in any other. Consequently, the regolith is shallow, being normally only 6 to 12 inches thick, but forms a complete covering; rock outcrops are virtually non-existent. Originally, the depth of the overburden must have been more variable; the present uniformity results from the fact that most basalt slopes are cultivated. The more rapid erosion in humid areas

[6]*Ibid.*

prevents the overburden from building up to a depth appreciably greater than is found in drier zones where weathering is slower.

In a strict sense, the BY soil is scarcely a soil at all. It consists merely of a layer of brown to grey-brown, stony, gravelly loam lying upon the bedrock from which it has been weathered. No evidence of profile development is to be seen. Yet, since the basalt contains significant quantities of both the potash-producing orthoclase and the phosphate-producing apatite, the surface material is fairly fertile. Because it forms such a thin layer, it is best used for shallow-rooted crops.

BM. *Mature soil on basalt*

The mature basalt soil is found only on the rock plain of the northeastern Plaine du Nord, where relief is low, the rainy season is short and there is a pronounced dry period (Climatic Type V). Natural vegetation is xerophytic forest.

The overburden is 12 to 36 inches or more in depth, and in most areas a complete profile has developed. An A horizon 6 to 18 inches deep of compact, dark reddish-brown clay loam overlies a 12 to 28 inch B horizon of red or red-brown silty clay loam, usually stony. The parent material consists of heavy yellow-brown stony clay. This soil is moderately to imperfectly drained, and has a good moisture-holding capacity, but has been severely leached. It is therefore less fertile than the BY soil, but is more suitable for deep-rooted crops.

ST. *Thin soil on shale, many outcrops*

This soil has developed on shale in areas of hilly to rolling relief and with a severe dry season (Climatic Types VI and VII). Short grasses with a few coniferous trees or xerophytic scrub from the natural vegetation.

In these areas no true soil, in fact, exists. The bedrock outcrops over a large part of the surface and is mantled by a weathered layer consisting, at most, of a few inches of grey-brown angular gravel. For cultivation, the land is almost worthless, and even as pasture it has very limited value.

Ss. *Shallow soil on shale, few outcrops*

Soil of this type has developed on shale in areas of low relief and low precipitation (Climate Type VI) or in areas of moderate relief and moderate precipitation (Climatic Type IV). Natural vegetation is mainly an open pine forest with grassy glades, though to the west, where the rainfall is a little heavier, some semi-deciduous trees are to be found.

Depth of the overburden ranges from 3 to 15 inches, but profile development is negligible. The entire soil zone is yellow-brown in colour and of a silt loam texture with or without an admixture of angular gravel. Below the soil the bedrock is greatly disintegrated for a foot or more in depth. With moderate to good drainage, and a good supply of most plant nutrients except potassium, this soil is of some value for agriculture despite its droughtiness.

S<small>D</small>.   *Deep soil on shale*

This important agricultural soil has developed in areas of level terrain and low precipitation (Climatic Type VI), in areas of level and rolling relief and moderate precipitation (Climatic Types II and III) and on all slopes in areas of high precipitation (Climatic Type I). Vegetation is usually semi-deciduous forest, though pines are occasionally found. In depth, the overburden is everywhere over 15 inches and commonly over 36 inches; the soil profile is well developed. An A horizon was found in two-thirds of the profiles of this type studied, and consists of a layer of brown or dark brown loam up to 18 inches deep. The B horizon is 9 to 15 inches deep and is a rather compact reddish-brown silt loam or silty clay, overlying a parent of orange-brown or orange-grey fine sandy loam. The profile is normally stone-free, and drainage is imperfect. The soil is well supplied with plant nutrients and, below the A horizon, is moderately to strongly acid.

L<small>H</small>.   *Shallow limestone hill soil*

This soil is found in discontinuous shallow pockets among outcrops of limestone in climates ranging from Type I to Type VI. Vegetation is broadleaf semi-deciduous forest.

In texture, the soil is a homogeneous, friable clay loam lying directly upon the smooth, evidently unweathered surface of the rock. The colour of the soil may be red or nearly black, depending on drainage, the red soil occupying the better drained sites. The pockets of soil are generally less than 10 inches deep. On many hillsides they are very sparsely distributed, and even on the best sites rock outcrops occupy over 50 per cent of the total surface area. Yet, despite its shallowness and discontinuity, the soil is quite fertile and moisture-retentive.

L<small>HD</small>.   *Deep limestone hill soil*

This soil is similar in physical characteristics and in fertility to that described above as the L<small>H</small> type, but it is deeper, with a maximum depth of about 20 inches and is therefore more useful. Where this soil is found, rock outcrops cover less than 50 per cent of the surface area.

LP. *Limestone plain soil*

This soil has developed on the limestone plains of the Central Plateau, in an area with a dry season of four to five months and a wet period of only three or four months duration. Vegetation is mainly a short grass savanna with scattered xerophytic trees.

This soil varies considerably in depth, ranging from 5 inches on the margins of the limestone plains to over 30 inches in some central sections. The deeper soils have an A horizon of dark brown friable sandy loam 7 to 9 inches deep overlying a 7- to 15-inch B horizon of compact red-brown gritty silty clay. The parent material is yellow-brown gritty silty clay, heavy and compact in its upper layers and becoming more friable with increasing depth, probably reflecting a higher lime content.

In many areas the A horizon has been removed by erosion, and shallow phases of the soil do not possess any C horizon, the B horizon resting directly upon bedrock. Drainage is moderate to imperfect. These soils are fairly fertile and, in their deeper phases, are especially well suited to sugar cane. Shallow phases, however, are of very little agricultural value.

Hs. *Shallow marlaceous soil with hardpan*

This is a poorly developed soil found in areas of low relief and a prolonged dry season (Climatic Type VII). Natural vegetation is xerophytic scrub or short grass savanna.

Drainage is imperfect, and the fluctuating water table has created a thick calcareous hardpan which lies often only 2 or 3 inches and never more than 6 inches below the surface. Above the hardpan is a very stony fine sandy loam, grey-brown to dark brown in colour.

Though the soil itself is quite fertile, the presence of the hardpan largely precludes cultivation.

Hd. *Deep marlaceous soil with hardpan*

This soil has developed in areas of level to depressional relief and with a prolonged dry season (Climatic Type VII). Natural vegetation is mainly semi-deciduous forest. The overburden may be as shallow as 12 or 15 inches, but more commonly exceeds 36 inches in depth.

The profile consists of an A horizon of black friable silt loam 8 to 18 inches deep which develops deep fissures during the dry season. The B horizon, of fairly compact dark brown loamy clay, is 6 to 15 inches in depth, and overlies a parent material of grey-orange, occasionally mottled, clay loam. A calcareous hardpan is encountered, immediately below the B horizon in some localities, but, more commonly, at various depths with the C horizon. Essentially the profile is stone-free, and drainage is moderate to imperfect.

This soil is well supplied with organic matter and plant nutrients and is potentially very productive.

H.   *Deep marlaceous soil without hardpan*

This soil has developed in areas of gentle relief but with good drainage, usually on low cols. The climate is mainly Type VI, with a pronounced dry season, but with a longer rainy period than in the areas where Hs and HD soils are found. Natural vegetation is semi-deciduous forest.

The profile is well drained, stone-free, and contains a 5- to 8-inch A horizon of black gravelly loam over a B horizon 8 to 12 inches in depth of yellow-brown sandy loam, occasionally gravelly. The parent material is a yellow-white calcareous silt loam or clay loam. Fewer soluble salts have accumuated in this soil than in the HD soil, and natural fertility is therefore not quite so high. Nevertheless, for all crops except root crops moderate to high yields may be obtained.

CG.   *Stony soil on conglomerate*

This material comprises the stony surface of the conglomerates of the Central Plateau and the northeastern Plaine du Nord. The climate in these areas is relatively dry (Types IV, V, and VII), and vegetation consists of an incomplete cover of short grasses with a few xerophytic and coniferous trees. CG soil is found on dissected sites from which any mature soil has been removed by erosion.

The parent material consists of gravel, pebbles, and small boulders, all very well rounded and compacted together. The only sign of profile development is a slight discoloration of the upper 5 or 6 inches, which are medium-brown to grey-brown in colour. The underlying material is a light yellow-grey. Individual stones appear fresh and show few signs of weathering. Apart from a little grazing, no agriculture is possible in this material.

CM.   *Mature soil on conglomerate*

Soil of this type has developed on conglomerate in areas of Type IV climate and remains on interfluves where it has escaped erosion. Natural vegetation consists of short grasses, forming a complete cover, and scattered xerophytic and semi-deciduous trees. Drainage is moderate to imperfect.

The soil profile is well developed, and the A horizon is generally still present in the form of 8 to 10 inches of dark brown silt loam. The B horizon consists of a layer of reddish-brown silt loam, 10 to 18 inches deep. Below this horizon one may find a parent material of yellow-brown silt, but more commonly the B lies directly upon a zone of well-rounded crystalline pebbles and boulders up to 6 inches in diameter. These stones are so severely weathered that they are easily sliced with a shovel. The thickness of the weathered boulder and pebble zone is at least 36 inches.

The surface soil is slightly calcareous and moderately fertile, only potassium being conspicuously deficient.

Rs.   *Shallow coral reef soil*
This soil has developed on the outer margin of the recently emerged coral reef in the northeastern corner of the Plaine du Nord. The climate is of Type V and the natural cover consists of xerophytic scrub forest.

Reef rocks occupy over 75 per cent of the surface area, but within and upon them have developed pockets of homogenous dark red-brown fine sandy loam up to 8 inches in depth. Drainage is moderate to imperfect. Although there is little soil, that which exists is quite fertile, and suitable for drought resistant crops such as sisal.

Rd.   *Deep coral reef soil*
This soil is found adjacent to the Rs soil and has developed under similar climatic and vegetational conditions. It is located, however, in the slightly depressed belt which runs just behind the outer margin of the reef and is much deeper than the Rs soil. Drainage is moderate.

Some profile development has taken place. There is a 15-inch surface horizon of reddish-brown loam overlying a brick-red fine sandy loam which continues unchanged until the reef rock is encountered at a depth of 30 to 40 inches. Many stones are found at the surface but few within the soil itself.

Chemically, the soil is similar to the Rs type, but agriculturally it is much more useful due to the greater depth and continuity of the overburden.

Rm.   *Mature coral reef soil*
This soil is found in association with Rs and Rd soils, occupying the higher sites where drainage is good to excessive.

The A horizon comprises 6 to 16 inches of grey-brown to dark brown sandy loam overlying a 16 to 28-inch B horizon of grey-white fine silty sand which is quite compact but which possesses a medium granular structure. The parent material is a yellow-white calcareous semi-consolidated silty fine sand which normally develops a hardpan on its upper surface, particularly if exposed through the removal of the solum by erosion. This material was observed in a quarry cut to continue with little change for depths of 8 to 10 feet. Of rather low fertility, this soil is agriculturally inferior to the RD soil.

SOILS OF THE UNCONSOLIDATED COASTAL PLAIN

Uc. *Clay*

Soil of this type has developed on uplifted mangrove swamps, in areas with a two- or three-month dry season and a wet period of five to seven months (Climatic Types IV and V). Natural vegetation is xerophytic forest.

Drainage is imperfect to poor, and only two horizons are distinguishable. The surface layer is 6 to 36 inches in depth and consists of a very dark brown or black hard compact loamy clay. Beneath it, the parent material is a massive yellow-brown clay with a relatively high content (about 10 per cent) of coarse quartz sand.

Chemically the parent material is neutral in reaction, very low in nitrogen, but fairly well supplied with other plant nutrients.

UCLW. *Well-drained clay loam*

Developed on alluvial and marine clay loam, this soil is found mainly in the humid western part of the Plaine du Nord (Climatic Types II and III), though it occurs as well in pockets to the east (Climatic Types IV and V). Natural vegetation is mainly broadleaf semi-deciduous forest.

The A horizon comprises 8 to 24 inches of dark brown to black clay loam overlying a 7 to 20-inch B horizon of brown loamy clay. The parent material is an orange-brown sandy clay. Drainage is moderate to good, moisture holding capacity is also good, and fertility is very high.

UCLI. *Imperfectly drained clay loam*

This soil has developed in places where the heavy clay of emerged mangrove swamps has been thinly covered with alluvium of somewhat lighter texture. It is found in climates ranging from Type II to Type V and under xerophytic or semi-deciduous forest.

In most profiles only two horizons may be distinguished. The surface soil, 8 to 36 inches in depth, consists of dark brown to black clay loam which lies directly upon parent material of yellow-brown silty clay. The soil is neutral in reaction and moderately fertile, but suffers from poor internal drainage.

Us-c.   *Sandy loam on clay*
Soil of this type has developed on alluvial sand overlying marine clay in
an area only slightly emerged from the sea at the mouth of the Rivière
Marion. Here the climate is of Type V, and the natural vegetation
consists of semi-deciduous broadleaf trees.

This is a young soil, profile development being restricted to a darkening of the upper half of the sandy surface layer. This layer has a total
depth of 8 to 12 inches, and overlies heavy grey and yellow, imperfectly-
drained clay. Drainage is imperfect, and fertility is moderate.

Usi.   *Silt*
This soil has developed on fine-textured alluvium on the margins of
some of the broader valleys. It is found only in the humid western
lowlands of the Département (Climatic Types I and II). Natural
vegetation is broadleaf forest.

This is a deep, moderately drained soil. It contains an A horizon
consisting of 14 to 36 inches or more of dark brown to black silt or silty
clay overlying a B horizon of brown or orange-brown silty clay. The
parent material could not be reached for examination.

The surface soil is mildly acidic, moisture-retentive, of high natural
fertility, and of great agricultural value.

Unsil.   *Silt loam*
Soil of this type has developed on alluvial and marine silty clay under a
variety of climates, ranging from Type I to Type V. Vegetation is
broadleaf forest.

The profile consists of an A horizon 6 to 24 inches thick of black silt
loam or loam overlaying a blue-grey silty clay B horizon of comparable
depth. The parent material is yellow-grey or grey-brown silt or silty clay.
Drainage is imperfect, but natural fertility and productivity are both very
high.

Ul-sis.   *Loam on silty sand*
This soil has developed on alluvial and marine sand overlain by alluvium
of finer texture. It is found in areas of Climatic Types I to V, near the
mouths of most of the larger streams entering the sea in the Département. Natural vegetation is broadleaf forest.

This is a deep soil, with an A horizon 10 to 27 inches in depth
composed of dark brown to black loam. The B horizon is 10 to 30
inches in thickness and of brown or dark brown silt loam, while the
parent material is a grey-brown or yellow-brown fine silty sand, in

places quite compact, and underlain at a depth of several feet by gravel. Drainage and moisture retention are both good, and fertility is high.

UFS.   *Fine sand*

Soil of this type has developed on recently emerged deltaic sand in areas with a two- to three-month dry season (Climatic Types IV and V). Vegetation is mainly xerophytic forest.

This is a very poorly developed soil; indeed virtually no profile formation was observed from the surface to depths of 36 inches. The overburden consists of a stone-free yellow-brown or grey-brown fine silty sand which has been compacted through the precipitation of salts carried upwards with the ground water during the dry season. Although no definite single layer of hardpan was detected, great difficulty was experienced in penetrating the soil with an auger.

This soil becomes exceedingly dessicated during the dry season, but it is often covered with water during wet weather due to slow internal and external drainage. Fertility is quite low.

USL-S.   *Sandy loam on sand*

This soil has developed on alluvial and marine sand without a covering of fine alluvium. It is found in areas of moderate precipitation and little or no dry period (Climatic Type III). Natural vegetation is broadleaf forest.

Drainage is good, and since the soil contains an adequate supply of moisture moving continually downwards, a very deep soil has developed. In fact, with a 36-inch auger it was not possible to reach even the B horizon. The A horizon, however, was found to be differentiated into an A^1 of 10 to 27 inches of dark brown to black sandy loam and an A^2 of dark grey-brown coarse sand with a small proportion of clay.

Chemically, the soil is neutral to slightly acid and very fertile. Its moisture-holding capacity is moderate.

USY.   *Youthful soil on sand*

This soil has developed on a recently emerged sand plain in areas with a five-month wet season and two- to three-month dry period (Climatic Type V). Natural vegetation is mainly xerophytic forest.

Although drainage is moderate to good, the profile has not had time to develop fully, and in most places only one weathered horizon may be distinguished, consisting of 12 to 36 inches or more of friable brown or dark brown loam. The parent material is yellow-brown or grey-brown medium-fine sand, often rather compact.

Chemically the surface soil is neutral in reaction and moderately fertile. Good yields are obtained from all except the most demanding crops, such as corn and bananas.

Usm. *Mature soil on sand*

This soil has developed under conditions similar to those of the Usy soil type but in areas which have been exposed to soil-forming processes for a longer time.

The profile consists of an A horizon of 7 to 20 inches of friable brown or dark brown loamy sand over a B horizon of 10 to 24 inches of red-brown sandy loam, and a C horizon of yellow-brown medium-fine sand. Drainage is good. The soil is slightly basic in reaction and very fertile.

Ub. *Marine beach*

This material consists of coarse sand and gravel of recent marine deposition with no profile development. Its agricultural value is very limited.

Ubr. *Raised gravel beach soils*

This soil has developed on raised gravel ridges in the eastern section of the Plaine du Nord, in an area with a two- to three-month dry season and a five-to seven-month wet period (Climatic Types IV and V). Natural vegetation is xerophytic scrub.

The profiile is poorly developed, consisting of a weathered layer 4 to 12 inches deep over unaltered grey-brown stratified coarse sand, gravel, and pebbles. The weathered layer is medium-brown or reddish-brown and somewhat heavier in texture than the parent, occasionally approximating a gravelly loam or even a loamy sand. Drainage is excessive, except in swales, where the mineral soil may be overlain by 10 to 18 inches of black loam or muck. Fertility is very low.

Uc-b. *Clay loam over beach deposits*

This soil has developed on marine sand beaches, uplifted and thinly covered with finer materials. Climate is of Type III and natural vegetation is broadleaf forest.

Drainage is good, and despite the relatively short period of soil formation there is a well-developed soil profile consisting of a dark brown, loamy A horizon, 5 to 15 inches deep, over a 5- to 17-inch B horizon of medium to dark brown clay loam. The B horizon may rest directly upon sand and gravel, or upon 7 to 18 inches of yellow-brown or orange-brown loam, below which the coarser materials are found.

The soil is neutral in reaction and moderately fertile, though deficient in nitrogen.

Uss.   *Saline sand*
A non-agricultural soil consisting of fine saline silty sand, this type is
found on the inner margins of mangrove swamps. Much of the area
falling within this category is inundated at high tide.

ORGANIC SOILS

WF.   *Fresh or brackish marsh*
These undifferentiated muck soils are found in coastal lagoons. They are
of little agricultural value unless drained.

WM.   *Mangrove swamp*
A non-agricultural soil, this type is constantly or intermittently submerged by the sea.

PIEDMONT SOILS

PF.   *Fine piedmont soils*
Soil of this type has developed on piedmont fans lying at the base of
basalt hills in areas of moderate to high precipitation and little or no dry
season (Climatic Types I to III). Natural vegetation is broadleaf forest.
Slopes range from 2 to 10 per cent, and the depth of the overburden
ranges from 24 inches to 30 feet or more. Numerous gullies are to be
found. Drainage, both external and internal, is good.
   The soil profile is not fully developed, indicating that the fans are still
being built up. Only one weathered layer may be distinguished, consisting of 10 to 36 inches of brown to very dark brown loamy material
which varies in texture from gravelly loam on the steeper slopes to silt
loam on more gentle gradients. The underlying parent material is a
yellow-brown or grey-brown sandy or loamy unstratified angular gravel.
This soil is very fertile and extremely productive.

PC.   *Coarse piedmont soil*
Soil of this type has developed on piedmont slopes at the base of basalt
hills in areas of moderate precipitation and a short but definite dry
season (Climatic Type IV). Natural vegetation is largely xerophytic
forest. Slopes are from 2 to 10 per cent, and drainage is good to
excessive.
   The profile is imperfectly developed; in many places the regolith is
undifferentiated, red-brown in colour, and composed mainly of angular
small stones and gravel in a matrix of fine silty sand. In other areas a
surface layer is present, not over 13 inches in depth, reddish-brown in

colour and ranging in texture from gravelly sand on steeper slopes to loamy sand on more gentle slopes.

The surface soil is neutral in reaction, and of only moderate fertility. Agriculturally it is much inferior to the PF soil.

ALLUVIAL SOILS

Fsi. *Flood plain silt*

Soils of this type are found in the flood plains of streams in humid mountain basins which drain southward by very low gradients and which have not been rejuvenated. The overburden consists of deep stone-free yellow-brown silts and silty clays, moderately to imperfectly drained and overlain by a solum of 6 to 10 inches of brown silt loam.

These soils are highly fertile and extremely productive.

Fs. *Flood plain sand*

This soil type is found in most of the stream valleys of the Département in areas which are inundated only after the heavy and prolonged rains associated with hurricanes. Alluvium here varies in texture from a fine sand to a sandy gravel while pebbles and boulders are usually to be encountered at depths ranging from a few inches to several feet. Drainage is normally good.

The only evidence of soil formation is that the upper 12 to 15 inches tend to be darker in colour and somewhat lighter in texture (loamy sand to clay loam) than the unweathered parent material.

The soil is mildly alkaline, very fertile, and highly productive for most crops.

FG. *Flood plain gravel*

Areas mapped in this category are those which are normally inundated by the flood waters of a stream after the violent rain of a thunderstorm. The surface of the ground is covered with rounded gravel and with boulders which may reach several feet in diameter. Despite its stoniness and low fertility, this soil is cultivated to a considerable extent because of the good supply of ground water close to the surface.

Ts. *Terrace sand*

This is an undifferentiated alluvial sand, standing above a rejuvenated stream, usually overlying beds of gravel, and well to excessively drained.

A slight colouring of the surface layers is the only evidence of weathering. The top 12 to 15 inches is usually a dark reddish-brown, while the underlying material is normally yellow-brown in colour. Fertility is variable, but in most places rather low.

TG. *Terrace gravel*

This soil type is found on stream terraces which have been moderately to severely dissected, and from which any original covering of sand has been eroded away.

On gully slopes no soil exists; gravel and rounded pebbles form the surface materials. Even on level stretches between gullies, the only evidence of profile development is some organic darkening and the presence of some loam in the upper 5 to 8 inches. Drainage is good, and fertility is low.

SUMMARY

The Département du Nord contains a great variety of soils, ranging from types which are extremely productive to those which are almost useless. In the formation of these soils, the influence of bedrock is, on the whole, greater than that of climate, since mature soils have, to a large degree, been destroyed by erosion. In most hilly areas, soil is being washed away as rapidly as it can be produced by the weathering of the parent material, and there is no time for the development of a profile in keeping with the movement of fluids in the soil and the soil temperature. In these areas, the main climatic influence on soils is exerted through the rate of disintegration of the bedrock rather than through the development of a soil profile.

Even on the plains, where erosion is less rapid and most soils contain profiles, many stretches of alluvial and marine deposition are too young to show the full edaphic effect of the climatic regime.

In most places, therefore, the structure of the Département, as reflected in the soil pattern, bears a close relation to the potential productivity of the land. While the influence of climate is expressed on a broad scale, many of the local variations in the agricultural landscape can only be explained in terms of landforms and rock types.

5. Geographic Regions

BEFORE PROCEEDING from the foregoing analysis of landforms, climate, and soils to the study of their relationships with land use and population distribution, it is necessary to subdivide the Département into regions of manageable size and some degree of homogeneity.

In making this subdivision, it is not possible to isolate areas which function as economic units. Such areas scarcely exist in the Département because of the prevailing system of land tenure. The economies of the most dissimilar areas are bound together by the activities of the thousands of farmers whose land holdings are fragmented and widely scattered. True functional boundaries, therefore, cannot be drawn.

Rather, the regional division adopted is the one which provides the most convenient frame of reference for an examination of the land use pattern. Natural vegetation and land use are considered as well as such physical qualities as relief, bedrock, soils, and climate. Where all of these are found to change within a narrow zone, regional boundaries are easily drawn. Where the areal limits of these elements do not coincide, the land use boundary is taken to be the most significant. Under these circumstances, land use deserves priority, for it is of a different order from the physical factors; standing beyond them, it is at once the measure and arbiter of their geographical significance.

It is impossible, of course, to ignore the question of size. Very complex areas cannot be subdivided indefinitely; one must eventually settle for a relatively low level of homogeneity. Also some small sections are different from surrounding territory yet too limited in extent to be classed as regions or even as regional outliers. These small areas must

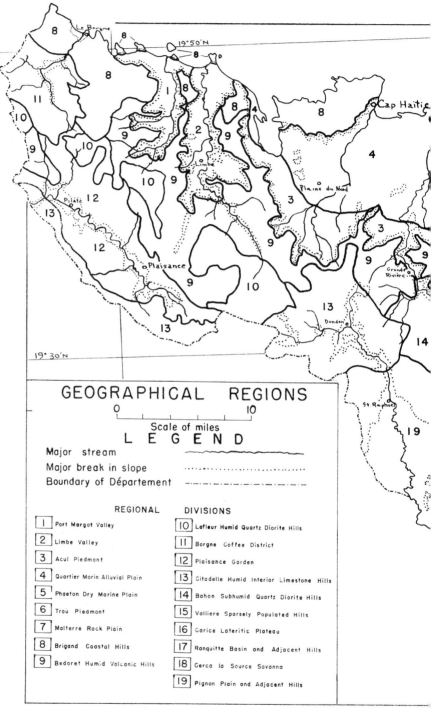

Figure 14. Geographical Regions

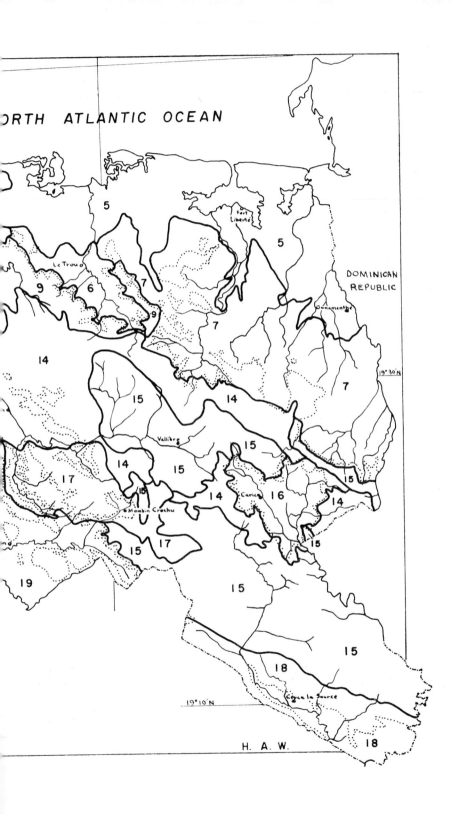

NORTH ATLANTIC OCEAN

5

Fort
Liberté

5

Le Trou

9   6   7

DOMINICAN
REPUBLIC

9

7

Ouanaminthe

14

7

19°30'N

15

14

Valliéres

14

15

17

14

15

15

15

Carice

16

14

15

Mombin Crochu

14

15

15

17

15

19

15

15

18

15

Cerca la Source

19°10'N

18

H. A. W.

be handled as best one may, by inclusion within a region which completely surrounds them, or, where they straddle regional boundaries, by placing them where the disharmony is least.

On the basis of these principles the following nineteen regions have been recognized, their distribution being shown in Figure 14.

Regions of the Plaine du Nord and other coastal lowlands

Humid: Port Margot Valley
     Limbé Valley
     Acul Piedmont
     Quartier Morin Alluvial Plain
     Trou Piedmont

Subhumid: Phaëton Dry Marine Plain
        Malterre Rock Plain

Regions of the Massif du Nord

Humid: Brigand Coastal Hills
     Bedoret Humid Volcanic Hills
     Lafleur Humid Quartz Diorite Hills
     Borgne Coffee District
     Plaisance Garden
     Citadelle Humid Interior Limestone Hills

Subhumid: Bahon Subhumid Quartz Diorite Hills
        Vallière Sparsely Populated Hills

Regions of the Interior Basins and Plateaus

Humid: Carice Lateritic Plateau

Subhumid: Ranquitte Basin and Adjacent Hills
        Cerca la Source Savanna
        Pignon Plain and Adjacent Hills

THE DIVISION INTO REGIONS

Perhaps the most clear-cut geographical contrasts within the Département are between areas with residual soils and those with soils developed on unconsolidated alluvial, colluvial, and marine material. The differences in the texture and depth of overburden are sufficient to bring about major differences in the types of crops grown and in the seasonality of production. Furthermore, soil boundaries also normally coincide with marked breaks in slope, while the slope differences in turn have a pronounced effect on the distribution of dwellings. Hence the line separating the mountains from the plains is taken as a regional boundary along most of the northern margin of the Massif du Nord. In the west, the Limbé and Port Margot valleys with their adjacent piedmont fans and coastal plains are quite distinct from the surrounding highlands and are sufficiently extensive to rank as separate regions. Eastward, from Acul Bay to just beyond Le Trou, the upper limit of the piedmont slopes continues to form an obviously satisfactory regional divide.

In the eastern third of the Département the situation is more complex. Here, where early coastal erosion carved a broad rock plain, the boundary between consolidated and unconsolidated deposits is not marked by any major break in slope, nor is the division between plain and hills one of great edaphic significance. Indeed, because of its involved geomorphic history, the northeastern corner of the Département presents a complex patchwork of contrasting land types and land uses which defies any attempt to delineate homogeneous areas of reasonable size.

The solution adopted here has been, in general, to draw a boundary between the area of consolidated and the area of unconsolidated surface deposits, for no other line based on physical factors follows so closely the division between agricultural and non-agricultural land. The emerged coral reef, however, has been placed with the unconsolidated deposits because, like them, it is mainly used for commercial agriculture. In effect, therefore, the regional boundary is here drawn between the plain of abrasion and the plain of deposition.

An additional boundary has been drawn to the south of the rock plain, dividing it from the Massif, but in this demaracation climate as well as relief is a criterion. Included within the rock plain area are a number of spurs, extending northwards from the Massif, and a number of isolated ridges which, in their rainfall regime and in their vegetation, more closely resemble the plain than the hills. The region of the rock plain and its associated hills has been given the appropriate name of one of its small villages, Malterre.

It is evident that, in the remainder of the Plaine du Nord, the differences in climate and in land use are sufficient to justify a subdivision into several regions. One conspicuously homogeneous area lies along the southwestern fringe of the plain within the areas of Climatic Types I and II. Here, where eight or more months of the year are wet, and not more than one is dry, the land supports a level of productivity and a density of population not to be encountered elsewhere on the plain. A regional boundary has thus been drawn roughly along the drier margin of the Type II climatic zone with minor adjustments being made to provide the closest adjustment to land use and soils. Since a large part of this most humid section of the Plaine du Nord lies, in fact, upon gentle piedmont slopes, and since the town of Acul du Nord is situated on these slopes, the region has been called the Acul Piedmont. It will be noted in Figure 14 that this region is not continuous but is divided by mountain spurs into a larger western and a smaller eastern section.

Farther east another regional boundary is drawn roughly between the area with a wet season of six to seven months (Climatic Types III and IV), and the area with a wet season of only five months (Climatic Type V). Here the more humid climate roughly coincides with an area of agriculturally favourable alluvium while the drier zone is occupied by less valuable marine gravels and heavy clays. It is not easy to say which is the more important, the climatic or the geomorphic divide, but the latter is generally followed because of its sharpness and its close correspondence with land use boundaries.

The drier part of the coastal plain which is thus separated out has been called the Phaëton Dry Marine Plain after a town which is the focal point of the sisal industry. In the more humid area to the west and south, two regions have been recognized because of differences in the texture of surface deposits, in relief and in land use. The more westerly region is flat-lying with mainly fine-textured deposits and contains much commercial agriculture; it has been called the Quartier Morin Alluvial Plain. Eastward, beyond a mountain spur, is a region of gently sloping, slightly dissected colluvial and alluvial deposits where the material is somewhat coarser in texture than in the Quartier Morin Alluvial Plain and where most of the land is in subsistence crops. This region has been named the Trou Piedmont, after its chief town.

The regional subdivision of the coastal lowlands now being complete, attention must be paid to the mountains and interior plains and basins of the Département. It is at once evident that the division between consolidated and unconsolidated material is no longer of value in drawing regional boundaries, for the unconsolidated areas, though important, are of quite limited extent. Prior consideration must therefore be given to other criteria.

The most important factor in the differentiation of this upland zone is undoubtedly the character of the bedrock. Because of the close relationship between bedrock and soil type, many geological boundaries are clearly reflected in the patterns of natural vegetation and land use. Therefore in the humid western hills several of the regional boundaries are geological.

To the northwest, the coastal hills of massive limestone form a distinct unit. Although this unit consists of several disconnected ridges, they are alike in having shallow pockets of soil, large areas in semi-deciduous forest, and small scattered populations. These limestone hills have been named the Brigand Coastal Hills, after their highest peak, Morne Brigand, which received its name not because of the character of its inhabitants but because of the difficulties involved in its ascent.

With this region have been included the small remnants of andesite and soft limestone which lie to the north, a narrow zone of basalt on the south flank of the Morne Haut du Cap, and a few patches of coastal sediments, all these being of too limited extent to be classed as separate regions.

A second region of massive limestone in the western section of the Massif includes a narrow strip along the southern boundary of the Département and a broader area in the vicinity of Christophe's Citadelle. In reality, this region is continuous, but part of it lies in the Département de l'Artibonite and it therefore appears in Figure 14 in two separate sections. It is somewhat less rugged than the Brigand Coastal Hills, possibly because the angle of dip of the rock strata is generally more gentle. It is also less homogeneous geologically. Between limestone ridges with relatively shallow soils lie deep basins eroded in belts of softer rock. The differentiation is important, for, while the ridges are sparsely settled, the basins are densely populated. This region is separated from limestone areas to the southeast on the basis of climate and agricultural intensity, and is called the Citadelle Humid Interior Limestone Hills.

Differing from the regions of massive limestone to the north and south, the core of the north-western highlands of the Département consists of quartz diorite, andesite, basalt, shale, and relatively soft limestone. Of these five rock types, only the quartz diorite forms in itself the basis for a regional subdivision. There are four major outcroppings of this rock, all forming mountain peaks, all with relatively poor soils, and all utilized at a low level of intensity. They are here referred to collectively as the Lafleur Humid Quartz Diorite Hills, receiving the name of their central peak.

Under the humid conditions prevailing here, the other four types of rock weather to form soils of comparable productivity. Land use boundaries therefore do not always coincide with geologic ones and may be more closely related to variations in climate or relief, as in the valley of the Trois Rivières. This valley is excavated primarily in shale but extends laterally on both sides into areas of andesitic bedrock. It is given physical unity by its relatively low relief and its climate, marked by ten wet and no dry months in an average year. Agriculturally it is an area of high and sustained production of a variety of crops and it supports a dense concentration of people. Consequently, the valley has been designated as a single region. It has been called the Plaisance Garden, after its chief town.

To the north and west of the Plaisance Garden, in the watershed of the Rivière du Borgne, is another region which is quite distinct agriculturally. Here, on steep slopes of shale and soft limestone, in an area where most months of the year are wet, coffee is grown on a major scale while cacao is also an important crop. This region is called the Borgne Coffee District.

The remaining parts of the northen and western section of the Massif are steeply sloping and of andesitic and basaltic rock. Although land uses in the two rock types are not identical, such differences as exist are relatively minor and have not been used as a basis for regional separation. The area is considered to be one region, despite its highly indented and somewhat fragmented shape. Called the Bedoret Humid Volcanic Hills, after a mountain on the Limbé-Plaisance road, this region is intermediate in land use intensity between the Plaisance Garden and the Borgne Coffee District on the one hand and the Brigand Coastal Hills and the Lafleur Humid Quartz Diorite Hills on the other. It is distinct from the Citadelle Humid Interior Limestone Hills because of its greater agricultural homogeneity, and from the Bahon Subhumid Quartz Diorite Hills, discussed below, because the two regions have different crop associations.

In the remainder of the Département, the southeast, the significance of geologic boundaries is somewhat overshadowed by the wide range of climatic conditions. From north to south the number of dry months increases from one to five. In some measure the climatic boundaries are related to geologic ones, but the relationship is not so close as to produce clearly defined regional patterns of land use and population density.

The section which stands out most distinctly is undoubtedly that which lies within the Central Plateau. The low relief, climatic uniformity, and distinctive soils and agriculture of this area set it apart as a geographic region. Included within it for convenience are several limestone hills, some centrally located, others on the fringe of the region. The region is called, after its largest town, the Pignon Plain and Adjacent Hills.

Another region which may be readily recognized is centred on the

Cerca la Source Basin in the southeast of the Département. Here the dry, dissected shale plain with its covering of bunch grasses and xerophytic scrub forms a landscape strikingly uniform over long distances and unlike any other part of the Département. This region is called the Cerca la Source Savanna. With it are included the alluvial terraces of the Rivière Océan and the north-facing slopes of the narrow limestone ridge which here forms the boundary of the Département.

Within the limits of the Massif proper are two other basins which, from the point of view of size, at least, appear to merit designation as geographic regions. The more westerly of the two, the Ranquitte Basin, has, however, been so deeply dissected that its soils are no deeper than those of the adjacent hillsides. Hence, the topographic boundary of the Basin is of minor geographical significance. More important is geologic differentiation within the Basin itself, the largest area of uniform bedrock being one of shale. This shale area, which is also the most densely populated part of the Basin, has therefore been joined with some adjacent shale hills to form a region called the Ranquitte Basin and Adjacent Hills.

Other sections of the Basin are underlain by quartz diorite, limestone, or quaternary gravel. Each of these sections has been attached to an adjacent region with which it is geologically similar.

In contrast, the more easterly basin, that of Carice, has been only lightly dissected and is much more homogeneous. It is unified not only in its relief, but also in its climate and soils. Lateritic soils cover most of the Basin floor, thus setting it apart from all other areas of comparable size in the Département. In addition, one finds within the Basin distinctive crop combinations and the most intensive farming within the eastern hills. A regional boundary has therefore been drawn more or less following the line of demarcation between hill slopes and the Basin floor. This region has been called the Carice Lateritic Plateau.

The remaining core of the eastern highlands has been divided into two regions, because the north and west differs climatically from the south and east. Different crops are grown in the two areas and the former, which is the more humid, is more densely populated than the latter. Also in the northwest most of the trees are of the broadleaf type whereas in the southeast most, though not all, are coniferous.

Yet, although climatic factors form the principal basis for the separation of the two regions, the boundary between them does not always follow climatic divides. In several places it has been drawn along the line between areas of granite and quartz diorite bedrock because of the sharp land use contrasts which exist here.

These last two regions are called, after their largest towns, the Bahon

Subhumid Quartz Diorite Hills and the Vallière Sparsely Populated Hills. Neither is wholly continuous. The former has outliers east and west of the Carice Basin. The latter includes two rain-shadow areas, one in the lee of the Cordillera Septentrional of the Dominican Republic, the other on the southern slopes of Morne Piton des Roches.

SUMMARY

Within the Département du Nord it is possible to distinguish nineteen geographic regions, of which eight depend for their identification on a wide range of criteria.

Of the remaining eleven, eight are distinct from adjacent regions mainly on the bases of landform and structure. The importance of these geologic elements, observed in the case of soils, is thus evident again at the regional level of generalization.

Climate is the primary criterion in the recognition of only three regions, all located in the dry southeast. Yet the importance of the amount and distribution of precipitation may also be indirectly perceived in the humid northwest. Although the regions here tend to be geologic units, their number and size are related to climate. Unless provided with sufficient rainfall, these small areas would not all have become important enough to be ranked as regions.

A more comprehensive evaluation of the influence of these physical elements upon the activities of man will be given when, within each of the regions, the uses of the land have been examined and analysed.

6. Rural Land Utilization and Settlement

AS SOILS REPRESENT the main link between parent materials and land use within the Département, so in land utilization itself we find the major meeting ground between all the physical elements of the environment on the one hand and the human elements on the other. Land use was seen to be the key to the demarcation of geographic regions; this is precisely because it is the factor of greatest significance to an understanding of human geography. Indeed, a study of land utilization must be an essential part of any investigation which is geographical in the fullest sense.

Nevertheless, within the Département, as in other parts of the humid tropics, the classification of land use, which must precede its analysis, presents some problems. Most fields are tiny, irregular in shape, ill-defined, and planted not in one crop but in several. In an area such as this, and on the scale which had to be used, no established classification scheme appeared to be suitable. Accordingly, a new classification was devised.[1]

In the land use classification which was developed for the Département, primary emphasis is placed upon the intensity of exploitation, as indicated by the percentage of land under cultivation in each area. Secondary factors are the types of crops[2] which dominate in agricultural

---

[1]Details of the land use classification are contained in the legend accompanying the land utilization map, Figure 18.

[2]A short description of the major crops of the Département and of their edaphic and climatic requirements appears in Appendix III.

areas and the vegetation of uncropped land in places where less than half of the land is cultivated.

Attention must also be paid to another aspect of the use of land, which is intimately associated with, and yet distinct from, its utilization for productive purposes, namely the functions and locations of buildings and built-up areas. Towns, villages, and markets are the subject of chapter VII, but rural farmsteads cannot be discussed except in connection with agricultural land and are treated in the present chapter. The distribution of farmsteads is indicated in Figure 19.[3]

The following discussion is based on the regions outlined in chapter V, since each region possesses some degree of uniformity in the use of the land or in the factors which govern its use.

Port Margot Valley

The most distinctive feature of agriculture in the Port Margot Valley is the hevea plantation which occupies about 2,000 acres, nearly one-third of the entire region (Plate 1). The continually humid climate of this area makes it suitable for rubber production, while the extensive sand plains provide the good drainage essential for hevea and the high fertility desirable if high yields are to be obtained. A few sections with silty soils are also used for rubber, but here artificial drainage has been necessary.

Most of the rubber trees are young, having been planted during the Second World War. Before 1953 production was insignificant, but since then about 200 metric tons have been produced each year, the yields being approximately 60 per cent of those commonly obtained in southeastern Asia. The latex is locally manufactured into crude rubber and exported through Cap Haitien.

With the exception of the coastal lagoons, the remainder of the region is completely cleared for cultivation, and a close relationship is seen between the type of crops grown and the texture and drainage of the soil. Flood-plain sand not used for rubber is mainly in rice (Plate 9), sugar cane and plantains, which are often grown in separate fields. Only one crop of rice per year is possible here, planting occurring in the fall and harvesting in the spring. Because of the relatively light summer rain and the open soils, rice is not grown at that season. Sugar cane and plantains, however, do well the year round as do such minor crops as corn and manioc. Actually, in more thoroughly drained parts

---

[3]In Figure 19, which carries the title "Population Distribution," the value of the dots is based on numbers of people, but their disposition is determined by the locations of rural dwellings.

of the plain, rice does not thrive even during the rainy season and is not grown at all.

Here and there in the sand plain one also finds a few coffee groves in which, as in most parts of the Département, the coffee is grown under shade trees. The trees most widely used for this purpose are the mango and the poisdoux (*tinga vera*), which produces a fruit relished by pigs. Also used for shade are oranges, avocadoes, and other fruit trees. Under the coffee, root crops are usually grown, particularly the shade-loving taro. In these groves, because of the deep shade and the dense vegetation, the soil is much richer in organic matter than in areas of open cultivation.

The largest area of coffee groves is on the northern margin of the sand plain where the soil is a loam over silty sand. This soil is extremely productive, and plantains are grown here as well as coffee. Sometimes the two crops are planted together in which case the plantains help to shade the coffee; sometimes they are set out in adjacent patches.

Within the gravel trains of the Rivière Port Margot and its main tributaries there exists a crop association which is found also in all other areas of similar morphology and materials in the Département. The main crops are corn and plantains, occupying about 60 per cent of the land while another 10 per cent is used for a great variety of crops, including manioc, taro, sugar cane, peas, beans, and tobacco. The stoniest sections, comprising about 30 per cent of the surface area, are grazed to some extent but have very little value even as pasture.

Because these gravel trains are subject to frequent floods which help maintain the relatively low level of soil fertility which exists, it is not necessary to let the land rest for any prolonged period. The floods may also destroy some of the crops, but in any one period of spate the channels of maximum velocity occupy relatively narrow bands within the flooded area. In intermediate zones, crops are usually unharmed except for young corn; this crop is therefore planted mainly between October and December towards the end of the hurricane season.

The reasons for the dominance of corn and plantains in the gravel trains seem to be, in the positive sense, that they are able to profit by the abundance of water not far from the surface and, on the negative side, that the popular root crops do not develop well in these coarse-textured materials.

On the fringes of the northern part of the region there are several imperfectly to poorly drained pockets of silt. These are used exclusively for rice, and because of the high water table at all seasons, two crops are produced annually. Some rice is also grown on the inner margins of the coastal lagoons in rotation with reeds, which here form the natural cover. Rice is planted during the period of maximum precipitation, when there is sufficient outflow of rain water from the land to freshen parts of the lagoons, while reeds[4] are grown during the drier part of the year when salinity is fairly high. Outer parts of the lagoons are never fresh enough for agriculture and remain in mangroves.

The remaining two land types of the region are the marine sand plains and the piedmont fans. Of these, the former is the less productive and the less intensively used. The sand of present and former beaches is of low fertility and rather excessively drained so that the main crops are the fairly tolerant sugar cane, manioc, and plantains, while minor crops include beans, corn and tobacco. Coconuts, which used to grow here, and for which the area is eminently suited physically, have been nearly wiped out by the bud-rot disease. There are also some fairly extensive abandoned cryptostegia plantations.

The piedmont fans, composed of well-drained material transported from weathering basalt slopes, are much more fertile than the beaches and are used mainly for sugar cane and plantains. Important secondary crops are corn and manioc, while some coffee and a great variety of food crops are also grown. Indeed, almost any tropical crop would do well in these fans, but sugar cane and plantains provide the most popular articles of food and drink in Haiti. Plantains, boiled when green, appear at every well-appointed table, and sugarcane is processed locally into syrup and rum. And though products for local consumption are important everywhere in the Département, they are particularly needed in this region to satisfy the requirements of the rubber workers.

The distribution of dwellings in the region is basically in response to two factors: moisture conditions and the plan of the rubber plantation. Peasant farmers invariably avoid depressional areas in the selection of building sites. Their homes are thus concentrated primarily on the marine sand plain and on the piedmont fans. Port Margot, the main town of the region, is also located on a piedmont fan. A secondary concentration of population is on an alluvial sand plain in the southern part of the region. Although this plain stands above the ordinary high water stages of the river, it is not entirely free from flooding. A few years ago, the one village of this area, Petit Bourg de Port Margot, was almost wiped out by the river.

The plantation workers have had less freedom in choosing where

[4]The main use made of the reeds is in the manufacture of mats for sleeping.

to build their dwellings, and most of them are built along one long road running the length of the rubber estate. Unfortunately, the road runs through the lower part of the flood plain in an area which will inevitably experience inundations from time to time. It is certain that the native people, left to themselves, would not have built their houses in this location.

Limbé Valley

The Limbé Valley is similar to the Port Margot Valley in its climate and in having soils developed mainly on alluvial sand and silt. The two regions, however, differ conspicuously in that the former possesses no large plantation devoted to export crops. In addition, there is a more subtle contrast between the peasant farms in the two valleys. In the Limbé Valley no large segment of the population consists of plantation workers who must be provided with food by the other inhabitants of the region. Consequently, on every farm in this valley, land not required to provide food for the farmer and his family may, if suitable, be planted in an export crop.

The crop most commonly grown for sale is coffee. Although prices fluctuate somewhat, there is always a market for coffee. Wherever soils are suitable—in those parts of the sand plain and the piedmont slopes which are neither imperfectly nor excessively drained—coffee is a major crop. It usually alternates with groves of plantains, and with scattered open fields of sugar cane and other crops (Plate 10).

Plantains and sugar cane, being more tolerant of indifferent moisture supplies than coffee, are also raised on the drier piedmont and sand plain sites, where corn and manioc are secondary crops, as well as on wetter sections of the sand plain, where they are grown in association with rice.

As in the Port Margot Valley, the region also contains pockets of silt where rice is grown to the exclusion of other crops and where two harvests per year are normally obtained. The rice is planted in small nurseries, between January and March and again between August and November. Later the young rice is transplanted into the fields, which are usually divided by low earthen dikes two feet high and three feet wide to give the farmer some control over the distribution of surface water. The dikes themselves produce crops of corn and plantains.

In the remainder of the Limbé Valley, the crop and land type associations are similar to those of the Port Margot Valley. Rice, reeds and mangroves occupy the lagoons; corn and plantains are found in the gravel trains; sugar cane, manioc, and plantains are major crops on the beaches.

In some respects also the two regions resemble one another in their population distribution. In the upper part of the Limbé Valley, floods are frequent, and the farmers build their houses mainly on piedmont slopes above high water levels as they do in the Port Margot region. Lower sections of the Limbé Valley, however, experience floods more rarely than do corresponding areas in the Port Margot Valley. The reason is that the flood plains of the Limbé system, unlike those of the Port Margot, extend inland for several miles south of the regional boundary. These flood plains in mountain gorges, being the first to be inundated, act as reservoirs regulating in some measure the flow of water downstream. One index of the difference between the two valleys is that on the Limbé the gravel train laid down in the zone of most violent stream flow dies away more than three miles from the sea, while the corresponding distance on the Port Margot is less than one mile. Houses may therefore be built with comparative safety on the flood plain near the mouth of the Limbé, and several dense concentrations of dwellings are found on higher sites. The largest concentration, including the village of Bas Limbé, stand on a former delta of the Limbé slightly to the east of the present river channel.

On the other hand, the town of Limbé, the largest settlement in the region and the second town in the Département, is located on the valley floor within the area subject to flooding. The reason for this location is that Limbé is more than a collection of farmers' huts. The town has an important commercial function, and has risen at the junction of a major north-south routeway following the valley and an east-west passage through low passes in the hills on either side. Because of the commercial advantages of the site, residents of the town have defied the river, but not without some cost to themselves. Most of the houses are built on masonry platforms two or three feet high to place them above the normal flood crests. In addition, several walls have been constructed to prevent flood waters from entering the town, but all have proven quite ineffective. If, as may well happen in the future, the main channel of the river changes its position and passes through the town itself, the cost will be much greater than it has been so far.

Acul Piedmont

This region is not quite so humid as the ones discussed above. The prevailing climate is Type II rather than Type I, and there is even a small area of Climatic Type III. Nevertheless, sufficient moisture for most crops is available throughout the year, and the land use here is similar to that of the Limbé Valley. As soils are less leached, their productivity is even higher than in the lowlands farther west.

Approximately one-third of the region consists of a gentle piedmont slope formed of materials weathered from volcanic rock. Most of this piedmont is used for coffee and plantains with the usual associated shade trees and root crops. West of Acul Bay, however, where the wet period is only about seven months in duration, the open soils of the piedmont will not support coffee, and the major agricultural emphasis is on plantains and sugar cane. Many other fairly tolerant secondary crops such as corn and manioc are also grown (Plates 2 and 11).

Below the piedmont lie areas of well-drained clay loam which are outstandingly productive, being extremely fertile and with such a high capacity for moisture retention that most crops may be planted in any month of the year, and good yields are obtained even in periods of drought. The main crops here are coffee and plantains, though some sections are in sugar cane and plantains.

The two crops last mentioned are also grown, and to a much greater extent, in some imperfectly drained, low-lying areas which have soils of clay loam, silt loam, and silt. These soils retain an adequate moisture content throughout the year, even without the benefit of shade, and are productive in all seasons. Despite the imperfect drainage, some coffee is also grown in these areas, though only on a few higher sites which are less affected by the widespread winter flooding.

The flooding, however, is beneficial to rice, and this crop even surpasses sugar cane and plantains in importance throughout the low-lying areas of silt and silt loam. Rice is the one crop to be affected by the seasonality of rainfall; it is planted here from October to December, at the beginning of the wet period, and harvested in the spring. Only one rice crop per year can be grown, and usually no second crop is planted during the summer. One reason is that the only peasant crops which could produce a harvest during the five months when rice is not in the ground are beans, corn, sweet potatoes, and various vegetables, but these plants prefer fairly well-drained land. Furthermore, almost all the farmers who have land on this part of the plain also own fields in the surrounding hills, and it is to the latter that most of their energies are devoted during the summer. Some transhumance is also practised; in the summer, animals are brought from the hills to graze on the fallow rice fields in the plain. Consequently, only about 60 per cent of this very rich land is in year-round cultivation.

In the eastern part of the region, in clay loam soils along the Milot-Cap Haitien road, accessibility to the port city has stimulated the development of several commercial plantations. Some produce sugar cane and plantains, while one is planted in grapefruit and another in sisal, even though the two latter crops do not really need such good land.

The presence of sisal in particular, represents an example of a lack of adjustment between plantation agriculture and the optimum use of land which will be dealt with more fully in the discussion of the next region.

Population densities within the Acul Piedmont are higher than in any other region of the Département. Nevertheless, a clear correlation exists between drainage and the location of houses. Most of the dwellings, and all of the towns, are on high ground free from flooding. Low-lying areas are relatively sparsely populated as are also the commercial plantations where, in general, people are not permitted to live.

Quartier Morin Alluvial Plain

This easily accessible region of level terrain and moderate precipitation contains a number of commercial plantations, of which the oldest and largest produces sugar. Climatically, this region is particularly well suited to sugar cane. The wet season of six to seven months duration is adequate for the growth of the cane, while the dry season of one to three months provides ideal harvesting conditions. Suitable soils are also found, the most valuable for sugar cane being the imperfectly drained clay loams, though some lighter soils are used as well.

Located just northwest of the village of Quartier Morin, the sugar plantation contains several square miles of cane fields and a refinery in which finished sugar is produced for domestic use and for export. A large amount of cane is also purchased from peasants who own land near the factory. As the cane is transported on carts drawn by donkeys or oxen it can be moved economically only about five miles. A new factory, recently constructed southeast of Limonade has made possible an extension of sugar cane acreage in that area.

A second important plantation crop is sisal, a plant which does not bring optimum returns from this good land. To explain the presence of sisal in this region, one must go back about thirty years to a period when a United States company acquired a large acreage in the region for the production of pineapples, and built a canning factory at Cap Haitien. The region is not unsuited edaphically or climatically to pineapples, and in addition to being close to Cap Haitien, it possessed a link with that town in the form of a narrow-gauge rail line which also ran to Grande Rivière and Bahon. After a few months of operation, however, the pineapple plant was closed, due to certain difficulties in international trade, and the land was allowed to revert to native food crops. The railway service was also discontinued and the tracks removed between Grande Rivière and Bahon. Foreign interests, however, still retained control of land and factory, and when, after the Second World War, there was a strong world demand for sisal, it was decided to commence production of this commodity. The factory was converted to handle sisal, and this crop was planted in the former pineapple fields as well as in additional land expropriated from the peasantry. To transport the sisal to Cap Haitien, the railway was revived.

From the point of view of the welfare of the native population, this move is difficult, if not impossible, to justify. The soil used for sisal is mainly clay loam, very fertile, and capable of producing high and sustained yields of much-needed food. As it is, food shortages are common all around the plantation area, while slightly to the east within the area of Climatic Type IV, they occur regularly every year. .The sisal workers must also face periods of extended unemployment when lowering world prices make it desirable for the plant to cease or curtail production. This enterprise operates at a relatively high cost, partly because of the lack of centrality of the factory and the fragmented distribution of the land holdings, and partly because, under the relatively humid conditions existing here, sisal does not produce the optimum amount of fibre. Consequently this plantation is unusually sensitive to external economic conditions.

A small banana plantation, a relic of the Second World War banana boom, still stands on the banks of the lower Grande Rivière. The fine deltaic sand of this area is not highly fertile, but the site was chosen because of its accessibility and because it can be easily irrigated. Water is pumped from the Grande Rivière, which here follows a fixed course, and it is possible to control the time of maturation of the fruit, an important consideration when exports are planned. No bananas are exported at present, but the output of the plantation finds a ready market in Cap Haitien and elsewhere locally. The author has no fault to find with this use of the land.

Turning now to peasant farming, one finds a closer relation between the crops grown and the physical potentialities of the land than in the case of plantation agriculture. In general, the southern and western margins of the Quartier Morin Alluvial Plain grow the same crops as the Acul Piedmont, though there is a slight increase in sugar production at the expense of plantains. The longer dry season and the less perfect drainage reduce the yields of the latter crop so that it is dominant only on the higher sites. The same factors also preclude all coffee production except in particularly fine soils on the banks of the Haut du Cap and Ste. Suzanne Rivers. Throughout this relatively humid belt, because of the good moisture retention of the soils, sugar cane, corn, vegetables, and root crops of all kinds may be planted in any season and usually give year-round yields.

Between Cap Haitien and the village of La Plaine du Nord, conditions are somewhat different. This part of the region is a low-lying zone in which sedimentation is still in progress. One section is a marsh, and another, above water most of the year, is usually flooded to a depth of a foot or so during the rainy season; both areas produce rice as a major crop. In the former it is planted alone or with reeds, and two crops are obtained annually. In the latter some sugar cane and plantains are also grown, though the plantains are often killed by the floods. Rice is also raised in several narrow lagoons on the inner margins of the coastal mangrove swamp, though because of the salinity of the water during the dry season only one crop per year is possible.

The northwestern part of the region differs again. Here several low basalt hills, with very thin soils, are joined to the Morne Haut du Cap by a raised gravel beach. Colluvial deposits surround these hills and mantle the base of the Morne Haut du Cap. Because this area is located in the rain-shadow of the mountain, the overburden has not been greatly weathered and is quite coarse. Soils are droughty and rather infertile, and are used largely for sisal. Manioc is also grown in considerable quantities since it requires good or excessive drainage and is rather indifferent to drought. On the piedmont slopes, some sugar cane and plantains are also found, but the former, in particular, does not thrive. Planting is carried out only during the rainy season, and food deficiencies are common. Some land, especially on the rock knobs, is in xerophytic scrub.

Along the eastern margin of the region, moisture is also deficient. The climate is mainly of Type IV, and most of the soil is developed on sand brought down by the Grande Rivière. Because of the low moisture-retention of the soil, even a short dry season one month in length has an adverse effect on agriculture, and a three-month dry period invariably brings food shortages. Throughout this area plantains and sugar cane continue to be the main crops, while corn, manioc, and vegetables are also grown. Planting is generally only possible during the wet season.

The great importance of soil texture in this area of marginal humidity can be clearly seen by comparing yields in the sand with those in the pockets of clay which are found here and there. In the clay, planting and harvesting proceed the year round, regardless of seasons.

Different from all other parts of the region are the coastal zones. Here may be found stretches of emerged marine sand plain, still somewhat saline, and also coarse deltaic and beach sands. In all these areas productivity is low and only about half the land is under cultivation at any one time. Sugar cane, manioc, and plantains, together with other food crops are planted, but yields are uncertain. Some stretches are in xerophytic scrub which is grazed by a few cattle and goats.

Beyond the sand plains and in swales between the beaches are flats which may or may not be exposed at low tide. Here grow mangroves in dense thickets, fifteen to twenty feet high. Where mangroves line the shore, contact between land and sea is so difficult as to be seldom attempted. But wherever breaks occur in the mangrove fringe, settlements are found. Some of these villages, such as Bord de Mer Limonade, are quite large, and all of them have a distinct economy. Fishing is an important activity, the catch being taken in traps woven from reeds. Another valuable marine product is coral rock, which is broken from the reefs at low tide and brought to the shore where it is burned to make lime for construction purposes. The necessary fuel is derived from the mangrove swamps, for the swamps are interrupted by many small inlets wide enough to take a boat, and at high tide wood may be removed quite easily. Not all the mangrove wood is used in lime-making; a good deal is sold as domestic fuel (Plate 19).

In addition to their maritime activities, the people who live by the sea also have gardens in which they raise most of their food, and where they work during the wet weather, when the sea is often stormy. There is no evidence of great prosperity in these coastal villages, mainly because the available agricultural land is usually poor, but there is at least the possibility of some year-round work and income.

For the region as a whole, the population is only moderately high. It is clear that an acre of sisal, and possibly even an acre of sugar cane, will not support as many people as an acre devoted entirely to food crops. The areas of commercial agriculture are blank, or nearly so, on the population map, and although people are concentrated around the boundaries of the plantations, their numbers are not large enough to bring the over-all population density anywhere near the level to be found in the Acul Piedmont. In shape the concentrations tend to be linear, following the roads, the largest lying along the eastern margin of the region while smaller ones are scattered west of the Quartier Morin. More people live around the sugar fields than in areas devoted to sisal.

An additional influence on population distribution is drainage. Few people live in the depressional area between the town of La Plaine du Nord and the Morne Haut du Cap, while those who farm this productive zone have their houses concentrated on the relatively infertile piedmont slope and marine beaches on the south flank of the mountain. A similar, though less striking correlation between settlement and drainage is seen in the southwestern part of the region. In contrast, the population is very evenly distributed in the southeast, where the land is all in subsistence crops and drainage is relatively good.

Phaëton Dry Marine Plain

This region is one of considerable physiographic diversity, but is unified by its generally low relief, its short wet season of only five or six months duration, and its dependence primarily on a single crop, sisal. This crop is grown on four estates, two of which are quite small and have only recently come into production.

The growth of sisal is favoured here by the accessibility of the region and by the fact that much of its soil is too poor to produce good yields of food crops under the prevailing climatic conditions. About half of the region consists of emerged coral reefs (Plate 12), marine beaches and mangrove swamps, and the soils which have developed on such sites are either shallow, rocky and droughty, or massive and poorly drained. Where they are not used for sisal, they are mainly in xerophytic forest or scrub, with a few scattered fields of manioc, castor plants, plantains, and beans, and support only a very low population. Hence the operation of sisal plantations in the region since 1927 has been beneficial to the country and to the local people.

Even sisal, however, is not entirely insensitive to soil conditions. In the shallow coral reef soils yields are very low, and many of the rockiest areas have been abandoned. Yields are also low in the gravel ridges and in the heavy clays of old mangrove swamps, though not so low as to make these areas uneconomic producers. On the other hand, the deep youthful coral reef soils and the mature coral reef soils are quite good, while the best soils used for sisal within the region are marine and deltaic sands.

All these different soils have been utilized for sisal, not merely because they are more or less suitable, but because they are found adjacent to the coast and, specifically, to the harbours provided by Fort Liberté Bay and Caracol Bay. Both bays are adequate for the shipping of sisal, which is non-perishable and can stand rough handling, and though, as a harbour, the former is infinitely the superior, factories were set up on the two harbours in the same year, and in both places the transfer of goods between ship and shore is effected by lighters. Because of the larger amount of land suitable for sisal around Fort

Liberté Bay, and because of the way in which the bay divides this area into a western and an eastern section, two factories, both belonging to the same company, are located on the shore of this body of water. Caracol Bay has only one.

Of two small new factories set up in the region, one is located about two miles northeast of Limonade, and the other is a mile south of Terrier Rouge. Neither has a direct harbour connection, and their products must be sent out by truck. Shipping costs will thus be slightly higher than for the large companies, but this expense is partly offset by the high yields obtained on the small plantations, which are located in areas of better soils than may be found along the coast. In general, however, it appears that the capacity of the land for sustained production of sisal has been somewhat overestimated. The plantations are slowly but continually expanding their holdings and also employ liberal amounts of commercial fertilizers; one thousand pounds per acre is usually applied after every crop. Nevertheless, the largest factories are capable of processing about twice as much sisal as they receive.

No serious difficulties are involved in the operation of the plantations. Labour is abundant, and most field work is carried out by contract. The young sisal is first started in nurseries and then transplanted to the fields. Three and a half to four years after transplanting, the sisal is ready for cutting, which is carried on at intervals for another three and a half to four years. At the end of this time the plants are removed. The land is then ploughed with heavy tractors and replanted. Planting is carried out in May and June, just after the first heavy rains; weeding takes place in the winter dry season and during the mid-summer period of minimum rainfall in July and August; cutting goes on throughout the year.

The sisal is carried to the factories in small diesel trains operating on tracks which may be moved from one part of the plantation to another. Power at Caracol Bay is obtained from steam engines using mangrove wood as fuel. At Fort Liberté Bay, which has few mangroves but is a major unloading point for tankers, fuel oil is used as a source of energy. Requirements of fresh water for processing are not beyond the capacity of wells and streams, and salt water is used in washing.

The fluctuating world demand for sisal produces some difficulties, but these can be met in part by accelerated activity during periods of high prices and a slackening of output when prices are low. Sisal lends itself to this practice more readily than most plantation crops as no ripening is involved. In the largest plantation, for example, high production during the period of high prices up to 1952 was accomplished by overcutting. Ideally, in any one year half the plants should be of producing age, three and a half to seven years old, while the other half are young plants growing to maturity. Yet, in 1949, 55 per cent of the planted acreage was cut over, and by 1952 the figure had risen to 63 per cent. These percentages suggest that in order to maintain production harvesting was extended to under-age and over-age plants, and this view is confirmed by the average-per-acre yield which dropped from 2,690 lbs. in 1949 to 1,655 lbs. in 1952. After 1952 prices began to fall, and it then became desirable to re-establish the optimum age-structure of the plantations during a period of relatively low production.

Such procedures, necessary though they may be, bring many problems to the native workers. Unlike labourers in the sisal and sugar estates of the Quartier Morin Alluvial Plain, the plantation workers of the Phaëton Dry Marine Plain have, for the most part, no private gardens to provide them with food. The land is too poor, and the labourers too many. Most food supplies must be purchased, and periods of unemployment or underemployment are times of hardship. Even normal seasonal reductions of the work force during March and again from September to November, when little planting or weeding are done, pose difficulties. Alternative paid employment is scarce, and farming activity is at a lull even in the food-producing parts of the region. Some folk try to raise a few goats or pigs, but these animals more often than not eventually find their way into the plantations, where they are killed for trespassing.

It is therefore nearly impossible for a single individual to be both a peasant farmer and a plantation worker. Nevertheless, the region contains sufficient land outside the plantations to support nearly as many of the former as the latter. The land, however, varies greatly in the number of people it can support.

The eastern margin of the region, adjacent to the Quartier Morin Alluvial Plain, is an area of excessively drained marine gravels and of imperfectly drained fine sand and heavy clay soils. Here population is relatively sparse. On scattered fields, the peasants raise a little sisal and some drought resistant food crops, but food shortages are frequent. Most of the land is still in xerophytic forest; its optimum use would be for sisal production on a commercial scale.

North of Le Trou, between Caracol Bay and Fort Liberté Bay, there is another strip of xerophytic forest interrupted by patches of cultivation (Plate 3). The soil here is sandy, better drained, and somewhat more fertile than the sand farther east, but it still becomes so thoroughly desiccated during the dry season that only quick-growing plants such as beans and sweet potatoes or drought-resistant crops such as manioc and peanuts give much hope of a harvest. Fertility is too low for corn, and few plantains survive the dry season. In a few spots along the river, sugar cane is grown, but the only crop produced extensively is sisal, which is taken in carts to the factories for sale. Such an arrangement is not really necessary for the operation of the factories as only about 10 per cent of their supplies comes from small farms. Nor is it an unmixed blessing for the peasants, many of whom planted sisal when the price per wagon load was U.S. $7, only to find, at harvest time, three and a half years later, that the price had dropped to U.S. $1.60. If the sisal plantations were to be extended into this area the results would probably be generally beneficial.

Eastward, in the alluvium of the Rivière Marion, conditions are somewhat better. Although the surface soil is still sandy and immature, the water table is fairly high, and most of this area has sufficient moisture for sugar cane and plantains. These are raised as major crops along with more tolerant plants such as manioc, peanuts, and tobacco. Sisal is grown as a cash crop up to a distance of about two miles from the main road.

Near Fort Liberté Bay, the Marion delta sand forms a thin veneer overlying heavy clay, and several sections are so poorly drained that they have been left in forest. At the mouths of the two main distributaries of the Marion, however, channels have been dug to serve as drainage ditches and also, during the dry weather, as irrigation canals. The land which has been improved in this way now produces rice, plantains, sugar cane, corn, sweet potatoes, and other food crops. While there is often not enough moisture to maintain production at a uniformly high level throughout the year, a greater difficulty is excessive water during the rainy season. Often all crops, even rice, are killed by floods in the more easterly of the two areas, near Fort Liberté. In the western irrigated area, a number of natural ponds, used as reservoirs, regulate the water supply to some extent, and conditions are rather more favourable.

Of all areas of peasant agriculture within the region, the most extensive and the most productive lies along the international boundary, south and east of the Fort Liberté sisal plantation. Some parts of this area consist of raised coral reefs or gravel bars, and on these droughty sites most of the land is in xerophytic scrub, but the greater part of the land is formed of the deltaic deposits of the Rivière Massacre and of its tributaries. Much of this material is quite fine-textured, and even on stretches of sand there has developed a loamy surface horizon with moderate water-retentive qualities. Drainage is better than in the Marion alluvia, and yet the ground water is not so far from the surface in the dry season as to be out of reach of most plants. The soils are not badly leached, and their fertility is very high.

These soils, indeed, are able to produce crops even under the rather stringent climatic limitations of the area. Most fields are planted each year or, on drier sites, every other year. Plantains and sugar cane are everywhere major crops, while much corn is grown on higher ground with heavy-textured soil, and manioc is plentiful on high sites with light soils. Secondary crops are more varied than in any other area in the Département, ranging from moisture-loving types such as taro and rice to more tolerant plants such as tobacco, manioc, and peanuts.

Not all of the Massacre plain is productive, however. Astride the international boundary is a useless area of mangrove swamp, surrounded by a belt which is somewhat less poorly drained but still of little value. This latter area is mainly in xerophytic forest, though it contains scattered plantings of rice, sisal, manioc, and plantains. Also generally unsuitable for agriculture is the gravel fan of the Massacre. The coarse materials of the fan are so sterile and excessively drained that they support only grasses and xerophytic scrub.

Population distribution in the Phaëton Dry Marine Plain is very irregular, as might be expected due to the division of the region into areas of plantations and areas of peasant farms. Yet the irregularity is compounded by the fact that the two major sisal companies pursue different policies with respect to the accommodation of their employees. The plantation around Fort Liberté Bay contains within its boundaries villages for its workers. Consequently, relatively few houses are found around the boundaries of the plantation. On the other hand, the smaller Caracol Bay plantation has no such facilities. All its workers must live outside the estate which is therefore fringed with labourers' huts. Other dwellings are clustered together in the coastal villages whose inhabitants gain their livelihood from fish, coral, mangroves, and agriculture. These villages are located near stream mouths, since only these locations possess both relative ease of access to the ocean and farmland of reasonable productivity.

The peasants of the region, tied neither to plantations nor to the ocean, display a more dispersed pattern of settlement, but one which is closely related to the productivity of the land and to drainage. These full-time farmers of their own land are most numerous in the Massacre Plain, where houses are uniformly distributed in the higher well-drained section, and grouped in distinct agglomerations in the lower, imperfectly drained zone. To illustrate, the village of Ferrier, in the latter area, is an isolated group of houses, located on a spur of uplifted coral reef. The land around Ferrier is intensively farmed, but, being subject to flooding, contains no houses. In contrast, the town of Ounamenthe, on a level sand plain which never floods, is so closely hemmed in on three sides by rural dwellings that it is not easy to draw the boundaries of the agglomeration.

In the Marion Plain, since the drainage is generally poorer than around the Massacre, the population density is not so high. Almost all the houses, furthermore, are located on high points which stand above flood level, the largest concentration of farmers' homes being in the town of Fort Liberté.

Westward, in the area north of Le Trou and Limonade, floods are not a problem, and dispersed settlement is possible. This is an area, however, where most of the land is rather poor and is devoted to commercial sisal production. It has, therefore, only a small number of peasant farmers.

Trou Piedmont

This region is one of transition. Here the crops of the subhumid plains gradually give way to those of the better watered hills, and sisal, grown commercially, disappears in favour of subsistence food crops. The region is unified less by its homogeneity than by the differences which exist between it and surrounding areas.

The northern margin of the region falls within Climatic Type IV, with a wet season one or two months longer than is generally found in the Phaëton Dry Marine Plain. The greater humidity offers prospects of a more fruitful agriculture than is possible farther north, but the fulfilment of this expectation is found to depend largely on the character of the soils.

In the piedmont slopes, where the soils are coarse-textured, excessively drained and of rather low fertility, conditions are not much better than in drier areas. Where food crops are grown, only relatively drought-resistant plants are to be found. Yields are uncertain, and in most places the land must be rested for two or three years after producing one crop of, say, plantains and one or two crops of sugar cane or manioc. On the most droughty sites much of the land is in xerophytic forest.

The crop which is best suited to this land is sisal, and it is satisfactory to note that a large section of the coarse-textured piedmont has been incorporated within the Caracol Bay sisal plantation, while other parts have been planted in sisal by peasant proprietors.

For a time, sisal was also the major crop in areas with other soil types of greater versatility. These include clay loams, silt loams, loams, and sandy loams developed on alluvial material as well as residual clay loam on inliers of basalt. All these soils are capable of producing reliable yields of most crops during the wet weather, and those which are heavier-textured can produce food at all seasons. Even in the sandy loam area it is possible to raise such crops as corn, rice, and sweet potatoes, planting being effected around the time of the heavy rains of September and harvesting at the beginning of the dry season in December or January. Less demanding plants such as sugar cane, plantains, manioc, peanuts, and tobacco may be planted in any month with rain and are harvested at various times throughout the year. Even some coffee can be grown.

In these areas sisal is clearly out of place, but happily, in most places its tenure of the land has been relatively short-lived. Few plantings have been made since sisal prices started to decline after 1952, and, on peasant holdings, sisal is now being replaced by other crops. If the price of sisal rises appreciably, it will, of course, be replanted, but only those sections of this better land which have been taken over by the Caracol Bay plantation seem destined to remain continuously in sisal.

The southern part of the Trou Piedmont has a Type III climate with little or no dry period. In response to the more humid conditions, the materials of the piedmont have broken down to a fairly fine texture and are not excessively droughty. The alluvial soils, which are fertile and quite well supplied with organic matter, generally retain an adequate moisture supply throughout the year. Consequently, the agricultural landscape has a rich and varied appearance. On the lower piedmont slopes and on most of the alluvial plain, sugar cane, coffee, and corn are the major crops, while plantains, rice, and tobacco are also grown. Almost all the land is in use each year, and food shortages are relatively rare.

Other crop associations are found in alluvial gravels and in the relatively coarse upper parts of the piedmont fans. The former, like other similar areas in the Département, are used primarily for corn and plantains. The latter grow sugar cane, manioc, and plantains on a seasonal basis.

Slightly less favourable are the basaltic soils, mainly because of the shallow depth of overburden and the impeded drainage. Where the rock is eighteen inches or more below the surface, most of the above-mentioned crops are grown, but where the overburden is shallower the land is used mainly for sugar cane and manioc together with a few beans and plantains.

The least productive soils of the region are coarse, sterile quartz sands developed on outcroppings of granite. These soils support a natural vegetation consisting mainly of grasses, and little agriculture apart from a few miserable patches of manioc and corn. Fortunately, the region contains only two granite areas, and both are quite small.

Population distribution in this region, outside the uninhabited area of commercial sisal production, is related mainly to the productivity of the land. More houses appear in the south than in the north, with particularly heavy concentrations on the lower parts of the piedmont slopes. Basalt areas have a relatively sparse population, while the areas of granite are almost devoid of people.

Since the Rivière du Trou is somewhat entrenched in the plain, it does not flood extensively, and drainage conditions are not such as to produce any nucleation in the settlement pattern. Indeed, the availability of water for domestic and other purposes makes it desirable to live near the stream, a fact which is reflected to some extent in the distribution of houses.

Malterre Rock Plain

This large region is characterized by a fair measure of climatic uniformity. The dry season is everywhere two to three months in length, and most of the region has six to seven wet months each year, though northern sections may have as few as five. Agricultural differentiation, therefore, is related less to climatic differences than to differences in bedrock and related soil types.

To the northeast is a zone of basalt hills and plains which falls mainly within Climatic Type V. Here the hills have very shallow and droughty soils. Their slopes are largely covered with xerophytic scrub, though, near the bottoms of some steep valleys, a few drought resistant crops are grown.

Because erosion in this area is slow, the hills are not surrounded by extensive piedmont fans, but merge rather abruptly with the surrounding basalt plain. Soils on the plain are heavier and deeper than in the hills, but its northern section has only five wet months a year and the only plant which seems to do well here is sisal. Some of this land has been incorporated within the Fort Liberté Bay plantation, and other sections produce sisal on peasant farms; in both cases high yields of fibre are obtained. Some manioc, plantains, castor beans, and other tolerant crops are found, but these plants will not produce a harvest in years of drought. Except in areas largely given over to sisal, xerophytic forest and scrub, supporting a few goats and cattle, form the dominant cover. Only about twenty per cent of the land is cultivated at any one time.

In the southern part of the basalt area, the wet season is one or two months longer than in the north, and agriculture is more fully established. Sugar cane, corn, manioc, and plantains, together with secondary crops, occupy 30 to 50 per cent of the land. Areas not in cultivation are pastured, and, although the landscape is not luxuriant, it is clearly one of farms rather than forests.

East of the basalt, and on the dry northern margin of the region, is an area of lightly dissected conglomerate. Over most of this area, rounded pebbles and gravel form the surface materials. Nothing will grow on the slopes and ridges except short bunch grasses, cacti and shrubs, while a few xerophytic trees occupy the valleys. Some cattle, goats and sheep are grazed, but this area is essentially an edaphic desert. Cultivation is restricted to a few marginal areas and depressions where the gravel is overlain by a light sandy wash and where a few plants of manioc, millet, and beans barely manage to survive.

The conglomerate zone also contains, however, limited patches of mature, fairly fertile, silt loam soils. These patches are found, moreover, in areas with a six- to seven-month wet season, and there seems to be no reason why they should not be agriculturally productive. Yet, at the present time, they are mainly in grassland, with or without a few groves of semi-deciduous trees and a few scattered fields of manioc and beans. Possibly, being surrounded by more or less worthless areas of similar outward appearance, these small sections with better soils have not yet been fully discovered by the local peasantry.

South of the basalt and conglomerate, granite and quartz diorite form the surface of the plain. Of these, the former is clearly the inferior from an agricultural point of view (Plate 4). Where the granite has not been dissected, sandy soils underlain by iron hardpan are widespread (Plate 13), and these are no better for farming than the stony soils of the conglomerate. Grasses alone occupy the ridges and slopes, while depressions contain a few shrubs. No cultivation is practised. As in the conglomerate, the interfluves contain limited areas of mature silty clay loam soil which is of some fertility. These soils could produce crops, especially with the addition of some nitrate, but are now generally unused except as pasture.

The only areas within the granite which are cultivated to any extent are the valleys. These are not particularly deep, but are fairly wide. They represent areas in which most of the overburden has been removed, the bedrock being covered by a shallow layer of freshly weathered material. Partly because this material has been less leached than the deeper soils, and partly because the water table is closer to the surface, the valleys have a natural cover of xerophytic scrub rather than grasses, and are preferred sites for cultivation. Manioc, beans, peanuts, and millet are almost the only crops, but they occupy 20 to 30 per cent of the land.

Within the area of quartz diorite are to be found soils which, though not outstanding from any objective viewpoint, are still better than most other soils of the region. The surface horizons are sufficiently fine-textured to retain some moisture in the dry season, fertility is moderate, and no hardpan is to be found. The best quartz diorite areas are those which contain well-developed valleys. The valleys are broad and shallow, and their bottoms and lower slopes are generally cultivated. Fairly demanding crops such as corn and sweet potatoes are found as well as the more tolerant manioc and plantains. Pasture and scrub forest tend to be restricted to the interfluves. Altogether, about 60 per cent of the land is in cultivation (Plate 14).

Undissected or lightly dissected quartz diorite sites are less valuable. The water table is farther from the surface, the soils are more leached, and conditions are similar to those in the better granitic areas. Some manioc and beans are raised, but most of the land is in xerophytic forest.

Agricultural conditions in the quartz diorite show some deterioration as one moves from south to north, doubtless reflecting the gradual reduction in the length of the wet season. However, even near Ounamenthe, it is clear that the land is of greater potential than the generally prevailing intensity of land use would lead one to believe. Its productive capacity has been demonstrated by the experience of an agricultural colony established at d'Osmond in 1937 to provide a home for refugees from the Dominican Republic. Working under the guidance of a trained agriculturist, the colonists, now numbering 925, have brought under cultivation 1,600 acres which were formerly in open pasture. A good deal of this land is on a sand plain which is part of the Phaëton Dry Marine Plain region, but a significant part, including an experimental farm, is on quartz diorite. Here manioc and peanuts do well and are able to survive any drought. Cabbages, corn, cotton, pineapples, oranges, and lemon grass have been successfully grown. A hybrid corn, maturing in three months, has also been a success. Producing a harvest even in poor years, this crop has been particularly valuable to the colonists.

The last section of the region to be discussed includes the spurs of granite and quartz diorite rock which extend northwards into the plain from the Massif. These ridges are very steep, their soils are shallow, and they are largely covered with forest. On lower slopes the forest is xerophytic, but near the crests there are some coniferous stands as well. Agriculture is limited in the granite to a few fields of manioc, beans and sisal, occupying barely 10 per cent of the total area. In the quartz diorite the soil is better, and about 30 per cent of the land is in crops. Corn, manioc, and even a little rice are grown.

For the region as a whole, the population is relatively sparse and widely scattered. The only area which can support a fairly dense concentration is the small, relatively humid part of the basalt plain, and even here some of the people need to obtain work in sisal fields outside the region. Somewhat poorer, but considerably more extensive, is the dissected quartz diorite area, which, therefore, contains the bulk of the region's people; their dwellings are quite uniformly spaced. Least desirable of all are the sections of granite and conglomerate; the few people who occupy these desolate areas tend to build their huts near to watercourses.

Brigand Coastal Hills

These great rugged ridges are formed for the most part of massive limestone in steeply dipping beds. Precipitation is generally adequate to maintain a cover of broadleaf forest, but soil is so scanty that a casual glance at the landscape reveals only a waste of pitted angular crags and boulders with a thin covering of low shrubs, tangled creepers, and scattered trees. From a distance, fields appear to be but polygons of rocks from which the vegetative cover has been removed. Only a close inspection will show the variety of crops which can be tucked away among the rocks. Guinea grass, manioc, beans, sweet potatoes, plantains, corn, and other plants find sustenance on shallow but fertile pockets of red loam. True, yields per acre are low, due to the large proportion of the surface occupied by rocks, yet the yields are fairly reliable. In many areas crop failures never occur.

It is generally true throughout the Département that, in times of drought, when all but the best soils of the plains are desiccated and nonproductive, harvests may still be taken from mountain slopes. This somewhat surprising fact was nowhere contradicted. All attributed the dry-weather yields of hill fields to moisture or "coolness" in the soil, a characteristic which, in turn, may be explained in terms of greater availability of water through its less deep vertical penetration in the mountains, or in terms of a greater dry-season supply of moisture from fog and dew. Agriculturally, therefore, mountains and plains are mutually complementary to some extent. It is a particular advantage for a farmer, and one which many enjoy, to have land in the plains, where he may work in the wet season, and also in the mountains, where he may labour during the dry period. Consequently, except on the steepest slopes, all the more accessible areas within the region, and especially those adjacent to lowlands, are farmed to capacity.

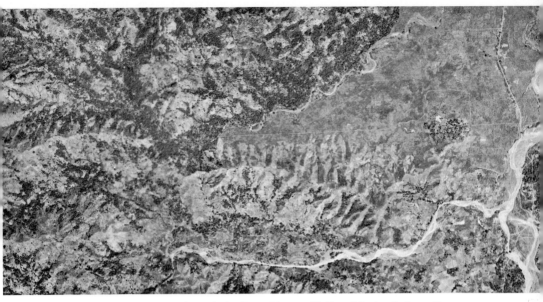

Plate 1. Southwestern Section of the Port Margot Valley. Much of the valley floor, planted with young rubber trees, appears a uniform light grey in contrast to the more heterogeneous areas of peasant farming. Hills of limestone in the north, of andesite in the west, and of basalt in the south-centre, differ in appearance due to their contrasts in land use. Note the broad gravel train on the Port Margot River. In the southeast is the town of Port Margot.

Plate 2. Hills and Plain South of Acul Bay. The Hills, of basalt, are greatly eroded but retain a thin covering of overburden. The plain, formed largely of material washed down from the hills, is fertile and well drained. Both areas are completely utilized, but the latter is the more intensively cultivated. In the northeast is a patch of mangrove swamp, while the town of Acul du Nord appears in the south-centre.

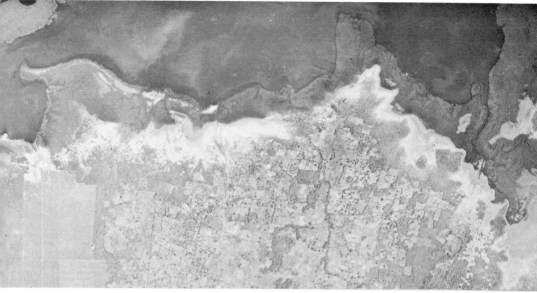

Plate 3. Coastal Strip South of Caracol Bay. In the west are fields of sisal and the Madras factory, while to the east patches of xerophytic scrub are intermingled with peasant fields. Northward, beyond white saline flats, are mangrove thickets. In the southeast may be seen the village of Jacquésy, where many houses are set in small clearings. Near the centre of the photograph, but almost invisible, is another village, Caracol, built on the margin of the salt flat. Passing through the area to the right of centre is the Rivière du Trou, much less conspicuous here than it is farther upstream.

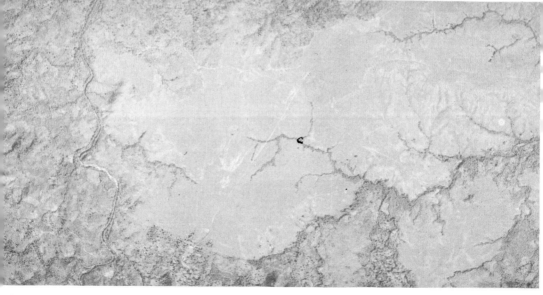

Plate 4. Granitic Section of the Malterre Rock Plain. The dissected area to the west, with shallow soils, supports some tree growth. In contrast, the less eroded area to the east, where the soils contain a lateritic hardpan, is covered only with coarse grasses. To the south, just left of centre, is the village of Acul Samedi.

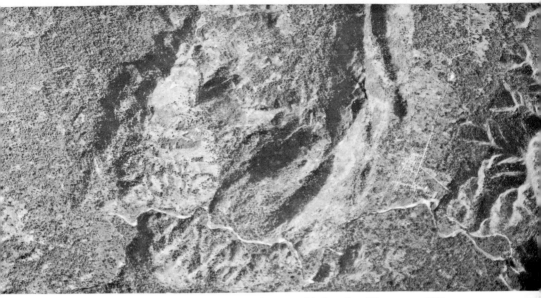

Plate 5. Hills and Basins of the Citadelle Humid Interior Limestone Hills Region. Trees in the basins are all of useful varieties, and land which appears to be forested is actually intensively farmed. The basin to the east, formed in shale and having heavy soils, contains many rice fields. At the southern end of this basin may be seen the town of Dondon beside the winding Bouyaha River.

Plate 6. A view of the Département's rugged centre, an intricately dissected area of quartz diorite. This area, typical of the Bahon Subhumid Region, is all cultivated, at least periodically, and supports over two hundred persons per square mile. Nevertheless, due to its poor soils and difficult terrain, it is one of the most inaccessible parts of the Département. The location is about four miles south-south-east of Ste. Suzanne.

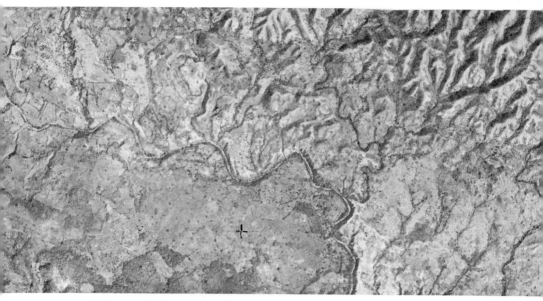

Plate 7. Valley of the Rivière Océan. The area northeast of the river is under-lain by shale, the area to the southwest by calcareous rock. Alluvial terraces of sand and gravel are found close to the stream. For climatic reasons, much of the land, especially in the shale section is not cultivated. In the extreme north-west is the town of Cerca la Source. A fault crosses the shale diagonally in the northeast.

Plate 8. Part of the Pignon Region. This view shows an area still retaining a remnant of the fine alluvial covering which once lay over most of the Central Plateau. Easily seen are the fences built to protect gardens from the livestock which graze in this relatively dry region. In the southwest is the town of Pignon, while immediately to the north a massive limestone hill rises over a thousand feet above the town.

Plate 9. Rice Fields of the Port Margot Valley. Here the soils are sandy, and rice can be grown only during the wet season; this photo, taken in July, shows fields lying idle after the harvest. Huts, surrounded by plantain trees and other plants requiring well-drained land, occupy low spurs which rise above flood level.

Plate 10. Here farmers are seen working with hoe and machete on a piedmont slope beside the Limbé Valley. Corn and beans have been planted in the field, while coffee grows under the mango trees in the background. The field has a slope of ten per cent, the surface soil is a well-drained clay loam, and basalt bedrock is encountered at a depth of 24 inches.

Plate 11. View over the Acul Piedmont towards Acul Bay. Most of the trees seen here are fruit-bearing and are used also to provide shade for coffee. Cleared sections of the plain are planted mainly in rice and sugar cane. In contrast, the basalt spur on the left is devoted to manioc and guinea grass.

Plate 12. Young sisal is seen here growing on the emerged coral reef which forms a broad plain between Fort Liberté Bay and the sea. The soil is fine-textured but less than eight inches in depth, and stones cover much of the surface of the ground. In such poor land even sisal grows with difficulty.

Plate 13. Outcropping of laterite near Acul Samedi. This layer of iron hardpan has developed in material weathered from granite bedrock. Note then that the vegetation consists only of short bunch grasses and low shrubs. The laterite is exposed here on the margin of a shallow valley.

Plate 14. Quartz Diorite Section of the Malterre Rock Plain. Here the soil is sufficiently deep and fine-textured to support a considerable amount of agriculture. All of the land in the broad valley has been cleared, and about half of it is in crops. The trees are mainly palms, mangoes, and cashews.

Plate 15. On this hill of basalt near Limbé, most of the land is used to produce manioc, sweet potatoes, or guinea grass. Slopes are from 40 to 70 per cent, depth to bedrock is six to twelve inches, but no outcrops or gullies are to be seen. The hill rises 1,300 feet above the sea, or 1,000 feet above the point where the photograph was taken.

Plate 16. This view southward across the Trois Rivières Valley shows rice and corn on the valley floor and on the shale slopes in the middle distance. Coffee grows at the base of the slope and also far up on the andesite hills in the background. Part of the Plaisance Garden region, this is one of the most productive areas of the Département.

Plate 17. Huge pine trees here rise in a parkland setting near Lamielle. In this area of granite, clearing of the land by fire has destroyed all young trees. No pine seedlings are able to establish themselves in competition with the coarse grasses which have sprung up.

Plate 18. Barren limestone hills near St. Raphaël. In this dry area, slopes so steep and rocky are not used for agriculture. Even guinea grass is not grown. In the foreground, the flood plain of the Bouyaha River supports a variety of useful plants including mangoes, plantains and sugar cane.

Plate 19. Typical coastal scene in the Quartier Morin Alluvial Plain. Fishing nets are hung up to dry, while at the feet of the women on the right may be seen part of the catch. On the left coral rock is drying before being burned for lime. Behind the coral is a heap of mangrove wood brought in by boat for fuel.

Plate 20. This view, east of Pignon, shows one of the few sections of the Central Plateau which still retains an undissected covering of fine alluvium. In this relatively dry area livestock graze freely, while a fence, erected to enclose a garden, appears at the left. Due to the lack of barbed wire, the fences are laboriously constructed of small poles.

Mountain fields must, however, be accessible, and in the Brigand Hills travel is slow and tedious. The ground is not only steeply sloping, but is covered with large and small solution-cavities separated by needle-sharp ridges and pinnacles of rock. No roads exist, and in many sections the terrain is impassable even for beasts of burden. The farmers struggle in on foot, and carry out their produce on their backs. Under such conditions, and in view of the small proportion of the total area which can be farmed, limits are set to the distance which peasants will travel into the region from outside. The limits, it would appear, are a mile or two in horizontal distance and about two thousand feet in vertical ascent; at greater distances from the plains, the intensity of land use decreases quite sharply.

It is, of course, possible to build homes in the limestone, but to do so does not really solve the problem of travel, for most peasants retain some economic, social and religious contacts with outside areas. Furthermore, in this jagged terrain, house sites are by no means easy to find. Consequently, dwellers within the region are few in number, except in a few areas with deeper soils. The ridge crests and areas adjacent to the most precipitous sections of the shore are virtually uninhabited and support a cover of dense broadleaf forest.

More favourable living conditions are offered along the coast, especially on the steep shores of Morne Haut du Cap and Morne Brigand where a few beaches exist, wide enough to support small villages. The people of these beaches have a way of life similar, but not identical, with that of the dwellers on the emerged shore east of Cap Haitien. Like them, they fish and farm and make lime, but their farming is more fruitful, as they have more fertile and more humid land to work with, and for lime they burn, not coral, but the superabundant limestone. Farming and the burning of lime actually make ideal complementary activities as the wood cut when a plot is cleared for crops provides fuel for converting some of the rocks, which are agricultural liabilities, into a saleable commodity. Small kilns are used for burning the lime, and no rocks need ever be carried more than fifty yards. Some lime is also made in this way by people who live inland, but production is concentrated along the coast because of the ease of water transportation to the main market in Cap Haitien.

These and other beaches along the submerged coast also possess some recreational possibilities. A road, barely passable for ordinary passenger cars, has been built linking Cap Haitien with two narrow beaches on the north side of the Morne Haut du Cap. On these beaches a few cottages have been built by urban residents. Farther west are several much finer beaches, but those closest to Cap Haitien are inaccessible for reasons of terrain, and those which can be reached by road are too distant to attract much attention. Recent talk of the construction of resort hotels has served only to bring about an increase in land prices.

Included within the region for convenience are several small areas of different morphology and soils. To the south of Morne Haut du Cap is a narrow band of basalt, where the soil cover, though shallow, is continuous and where guinea grass and manioc are the main crops. North of Morne Brigand are outcroppings of a soft impure limestone where the cover of overburden is not only complete but 18 to 24 inches in depth, about three times as thick as the basalt regolith. Here, and on adjacent piedmont slopes, there is a luxuriant growth of plantains, corn, taro, and sugar cane with some coffee and cacao as well.

Also north of Morne Brigand are some small peninsulas and islands of andesitic rock. These isolated areas receive relatively little rain, soils are rather shallow, and much of the land is in scrub forest, though corn and coffee are grown. To the west of Le Borgne, andesite outcrops on the flank of the main mountain ridge. Here more moisture is received directly from rain and indirectly as runoff from the upper slopes; most of the land is in use, guinea grass, corn, and beans being major crops.

At the mouth of the Rivière du Borgne a small lagoon produces rice and reeds. In a small sand plain adjacent to the lagoon, sugar cane is grown.

As was indicated above, many of the people who work within the region live outside its boundaries. In Morne Haut du Cap, apart from the small villages on the beaches, a concentration of dwellings is to be found only on the hills behind Cap Haitien, and even here most of the buildings are on basalt rather than on limestone. On the whole, the region is one of conspicuously low population. Only the outcroppings of soft limestone and volcanic rock near Le Borgne support a relatively dense population distributed over an area of any size.

Bedoret Humid Volcanic Hills

This region includes a wider range of climates than any other within the Département. In the west, most of the year is humid, whereas to the east, only six months are wet and two are classed as dry. Nevertheless, throughout this range of climates similar crops are to be found. All the land is in agricultural use, and the landscape is relatively uniform in its outward appearance.

This uniformity is the result, essentially, of the rapid weathering within the basalt and andesite bedrock, and of the severity of sheet erosion in the fine-textured overburden, once the land has been cleared.

Fortunately, the rate of rock disintegration is no less rapid than the rate of soil removal. Consequently, a layer of unconsolidated residual material overlies the bedrock in virtually all parts of the region. The hillsides are remarkably smooth, without any gullies or rock outcrops, despite gradients which most commonly fall within the range of 60 to 70 per cent (Plate 15).

Nevertheless, as indicated in the discussion of soil formation, basalt erodes even more rapidly than andesite. Piedmont fans are more fully developed below hills of basalt than of andesite. Rivers can carve broader flood plains in the former than in the latter. On basalt slopes the overburden in most places is only 6 to 12 inches deep whereas in andesite the depth is 48 to 60 inches. The basalt also breaks down completely, giving rise to a sharp contrast between solid bedrock and overburden, while the andesite, which disintegrates differentially, contains a deep weathered zone of loose rock particles. The overburden and soil developed on basalt are therefore unable to retain as large a supply of moisture and plant nutrients as the materials developed on andesite.

Despite these differences, the most extensive single crop on both types of rock is guinea grass. This crop fits ideally into a rotation system, for not only is it conserving of soil, but, once planted, it has remarkable regenerative powers. Even if it has been cleared from the land by burning, and weeded out during two or three years while food crops are planted, the guinea grass springs up again when the land is left to itself and chokes out other growth. Within the region it is most commonly found on the steepest slopes and near the summits of hills, where the soil tends to be somewhat shallower and more droughty than elsewhere and a longer rest period is needed for the land. Guinea grass occupies a greater area, proportionally, in basalt than in andesite soils; in the former some sections are kept permanently in guinea grass, whereas in the latter it is found only as a rotation crop.

Although one use of the guinea grass is to make thatch for dwellings, its greater value is as forage for livestock, principally cattle. These animals are highly prized. Their meat and milk provide a valuable supplement for the largely vegetable diet of the peasants. Nevertheless, they are raised only with difficulty since the hill slopes have neither fences nor water. Because of the lack of fencing, the animals must be tethered to prevent their trespassing among food crops, and this limitation on the areas which can be grazed by each animal necessitates their relocation at frequent intervals. The lack of water means that all supplies of this essential fluid must be carried to the high pastures from streams in the valleys far below. One farmer who was interviewed climbs a 1,000-foot hill three times daily to move his cattle from place to place and to provide water for them. For these reasons, the number of livestock raised in the region is somewhat smaller than the acreage in guinea grass would lead one to expect.

While pastoral management is, therefore, rather primitive, it is difficult to see where improvements could be made. Wood for fencing is in short supply, fence posts are attacked by insects and do not last long, and, in the basalt, there is not enough overburden to hold a post upright. The introduction of imported fencing material or the piping of water up the hills would be uneconomic. At present, therefore, the cattle population, while not pressing upon the carrying capacity of the land, is limited by the availability of human time and energy.

Grown in rotation with guinea grass on upper basalt slopes are two main crops, usually planted separately: manioc and sweet potatoes. The latter, being more demanding, is usually planted first, on freshly rested land, to be replaced after a year by manioc. Manioc occupies the ground for two years, after which guinea grass is allowed to regenerate and to remain for at least two more years before the cycle begins again.

On lower basalt slopes, the overburden is somewhat deeper and a shorter rest period is required. Less guinea grass is grown, and, instead, a greater variety of food crops. Corn, beans, sugar cane, plantains, and yams are planted as well as the manioc and sweet potatoes. The best land is never used for guinea grass, but is allowed periodically to rest for a year or so, during which period shrubs and short grasses spring up. If, as usually happens, the land is grazed at this time, an interesting vegetative selection occurs. Of all the shrubs which grow here, only the guava is not palatable to cattle, and in grazed fields the vegetation commonly consists of nothing save short grasses and guava bushes. Cultivation is usually resumed, however, before the guavas are old enough to bear fruit.

Most areas of andesite have rich youthful soils, which are used not for manioc and sweet potatoes, but for corn and beans together with plantains and upland rice. There are, however, patches of less fertile lateritic soils. These occur on the crest of the northern ridge of the Massif and in areas of volcanic ash, which weathers even more rapidly than the andesite rock. In these lateritic soils, rice is the major crop because of its tolerance of low fertility.

Some attempt is made on the andesite slopes to check sheet erosion. Here and there stakes are driven into the hillsides and are used to support low retaining walls of loose brush. These measures are not particularly effective but that the attempt is made here, rather than in the basalt where erosion is more severe, reflects the greater value attached to the areas of andesite and the greater ease in affixing stakes in the ground.

An additional crop in both basalt and andesite areas is coffee. Coffee requires relatively deep soils and is therefore restricted to the lower slopes of valleys in basalt, whereas in andesite areas it can be grown on any slope with a gradient of less than about 50 per cent. The location of coffee groves is also influenced, in the southern section of the region, by exposure. This southern area receives the greater part of its rain in the summer and experiences a moisture deficiency in winter. Hence most of the coffee is found on north-facing slopes which have the maximum amount of winter orographic precipitation and the minimum insolation at that season. In contrast, the northern part of the region receives rain both in summer and in winter, and here coffee is grown on south-facing as well as north-facing slopes.

The crops grown with coffee, as well as the sites used, are not identical in the two types of bedrock in the region. In the basalt, coffee is found in association not only with some of the usual shade trees and root crops, but also with plantains. One reason for this association is that, in the basalt, plantains only thrive in land which is also suitable for coffee. Also, because of the relatively shallow soils of these areas, the ordinary shade trees are rather stunted and the plantains perform a useful function in helping to protect the coffee from the sun.

In the andesite, on the other hand, plantains are seldom found in the coffee groves, not because they would not grow there, but because so much of the andesite soil is suitable for plantains that there is no necessity for planting them with coffee. Other trees provide ample shade, and because of the differing life spans and harvest seasons of the two crops, some economic advantage results from growing them separately. Actually, coffee was once somewhat more widely grown in the region than at present, particularly around the Limbé Valley. In the abortive wartime attempt to grow cryptostegia here, much of the coffee was removed, together with the shade trees which made production of this crop possible. Unfortunately few of the coffee groves have been re-established. Because of the time which it takes for coffee and shade trees to grow, and because of the urgent need for food, the land has been replanted in other crops.

Differing from the rest of the region, but included within it for cartographic convenience, are a few hills of quartz diorite, shale, and limestone adjacent to the Grande Rivière valley. Here the soil is rather poor, and less than half of the land is in use at any one time. Main crops in the quartz diorite areas are corn, manioc, and rice, while in the sections of sedimentary rock guinea grass and manioc are grown.

Population distribution within the region is influenced to a large degree by the paucity of suitable sites for houses. On these smooth steep slopes the creation of an artificial shelf on which to build a house is difficult in andesite and more or less impossible for the natives in areas of basalt. Consequently houses tend to be located either near the floors of valleys or, to a smaller degree, on ridge tops and spurs. In the central and southern parts of the region this tendency produces a striking pattern on the population map. Ribbons of dense population follow all the major river valleys, while secondary concentrations are found on tributary streams. A fair number of dwellings are also perched between the streams along the water partings. The northern parts of the region on the other hand, being surrounded by lowlands, are almost uninhabited. The land is worked by people who make their homes on the plains below or in the piedmont slopes.

Lafleur Humid Quartz Diorite Hills

These high ridges are agriculturally inferior to surrounding regions because of their rather sterile soils. The overburden is quite deep, generally exceding two feet in depth and reaching ten feet or more on the peaks, where a lateritic soil still remains. Nevertheless, the maturity of the soil is in many respects more of a disadvantage than an advantage, as even the small legacy of plant nutrients provided by the disintegration of the bedrock has been leached away by the heavy rains which occur in almost every month.

Consequently, considerable portions of the region are still almost untouched by cultivation. The highest peaks, rising above 3,000 feet, are the least fertile, the least accessible, and the least used areas. Few people find it worth-while to attempt farming here, and most of the land is in rather open mixed forest or grassland.

Lower elevations are used to produce some manioc and rice, which have low fertility requirements. Moisture is adequate, especially during the winter, for one crop of rice per year, and drainage is sufficiently thorough for manioc. A few other crops such as beans and corn are also planted, but after a year or two of cultivation the fields must be rested for three or four years. Furthermore, because the overburden is deep, gullies of considerable size may develop where the land is unwisely used. These gullies are not numerous, but a certain amount of land has been ruined in this way.

In a few valleys of the region some coffee is also grown. As in the southern part of the Bedoret Humid Volcanic Hills, most of the groves are on north-facing slopes. The soil fertility is so low that plantains are not grown with the coffee.

Population within the region is related in part to elevation, very few houses being located at altitudes exceeding 2,300 feet. Even below this level, however, population is quite sparse. Few house sites are available on the slopes, and dwellings are fairly equally divided between valley and ridge locations.

Borgne Coffee District

This region is the most homogeneous and one of the most densely populated in the Département. The entire area is humid, with a Type I climate, though a period of minimum precipitation occurs from January to March due to the interception of some of the relief rain by Morne Brigand. Steep slopes are found throughout virtually the entire region, yet because the bedrock consists of rapidly eroding shale and soft limestone, the slopes are clothed with a deep layer of overburden. Soils are fertile, their high potassium content and slight acidity being particularly beneficial to coffee.

Because physical conditions are so favourable for production of this valuable, easily marketed crop, and because the Borgne valley provides an easy outlet to the sea for the products of the region, the whole region is practically one huge coffee grove. On lower slopes some cacao is grown, and the food crops raised include plantains, corn, taro, rice, and sweet potatoes, but all of these are either found with the coffee or in small isolated patches. From a hilltop the region appears to be an almost unbroken expanse of dark green treetops.

There are only three small areas within the region which fail to convey to the observer a sensation of rich and powerful growth. One is the flood plain of the Rivière du Borgne, which is mainly in plantains and corn with a little rice, sugar cane, and sweet potatoes. Another includes a few low shale spurs, adjacent to the river and immediately to the lee of Morne Brigand. Here less rain falls than elsewhere in the region, and the land is used for manioc, sugar cane, and guinea grass. The third zone of low productivity is the crest of a limestone ridge on the eastern boundary of the region. Soils here are thin and stony, and guinea grass and manioc are major crops. These three sections, however, comprise less than 10 per cent of the total area of the region.

Because of the high productivity of the region, its population is very dense. Dwellings are also very evenly distributed. Some concentrations of huts are seen along the bank of the river, but equal densities occur on steep slopes at elevations of two thousand feet. Unlike conditions in the more uniform volcanic rock of other parts of the Département, the slopes eroded in these steeply dipping sediments are not smooth but consist of a series of low escarpments and narrow rock terraces which afford excellent sites for dwellings. There are also many permanent mountain streams so that the provision of water is no major problem. People live on the land they cultivate, and the homogeneity of the agricultural pattern is reflected in an equal uniformity in the distribution of houses.

In the northeast, where the rainfall and the productivity of the land drop below the regional averages, a lower population density is found, but, on the whole, no other region within the Département is as uniformly settled.

Plaisance Garden

Acre for acre, this region is one of the most productive areas within the Département. It consists of a broad valley, excavated in shale and andesite by the Trois Rivières, which has here reached the stage of early maturity.

Like the Borgne Coffee District, the Plaisance Garden lies entirely within the area of Climatic Type I. It does not receive quite as much rainfall as the former region, especially during the winter, yet shortages of moisture are rare throughout most of the valley because gradients are relatively low and soils are fairly heavy-textured. Consequently there is more vertical penetration of moisture than in most upland areas, and much of the water is retained in the surface horizons.

An additional factor helping to maintain an adequate supply of moisture throughout the year is the prevalence of early morning fog. Cool air desecending into the valley from the surrounding hills cannot escape, and commonly produces a thick blanket of radiation fog which is frequently so wet that inhabitants refer to it as a "little rain, before sunrise." Though the fog may form during any season of the year, it occurs most regularly during the winter period of minimum precipitation.

Only one part of the region has insufficient moisture for the most demanding crops. This section comprises the extreme northwestern part of the valley, in the rain-shadow of all the mountains between Pilate and the sea. Outside of this relatively small area, agriculture is limited not by climate, but, to some extent, by soils.

In much of the region the soils have developed on shale. Though these soils are not deep and are deficient in potassium, they have adequate supplies of nitrate and phosphorus. These characteristics, together with the slight acidity of the soils, come close to satisfying the specific requirements of corn and also meet the needs of less demanding crops such as rice. On the other hand, the typical shale soil of the region is not well suited chemically to coffee and is rather too shallow for plantains.

Occupying nearly as extensive an area within the valley as the shale soils are soils developed on andesite. Most widespread is the deep, fertile, youthful soil in which almost any crop will produce high yields, though, on some of the higher elevations, excessively drained and highly leached lateritic soils still remain.

In response to these broad climatic and edaphic conditions, there has developed in the region a distinct agricultural pattern. The major portion of the shale area, which is more or less humid throughout the year, is in rice. This crop is planted in early spring, before the heavy rains of April, May, and June, and is harvested in the late fall. In midsummer the rice forms quite a spectacular sight as a great pale green expanse of grain, devoid of visible field divisions, plunges into the depressions and sweeps over the ridges of this rolling country. On better drained sites much corn and coffee are also grown, though the latter is restricted in its occurrence to north-facing slopes, where it is commonly found in association with taro and plantains (Plate 16). These sites are preferred for coffee because their soils are deeper and more fertile than other shale soils in the region and approximate to those of the Borgne Coffee District.

Throughout the humid shale area no land is unused for more than a few weeks or months at a time, and food is available at all seasons of the year.

The region's northwestern section, which has a winter moisture deficiency, is also an area of shale. Here the soil is somewhat shallower and more droughty than elsewhere within the region, and coffee virtually disappears from the agricultural scene, while rice and plantains are found only in depressions. A little manioc and beans may be seen on drier ridge sites, but the main crop, occupying about half of all the land, is corn.

Those parts of the region which are underlain by andesite have more fertile soils than the areas of shale. Consequently coffee and its associated crops are grown almost exclusively over large areas of andesite, notably along the north-facing slope of the escarpment which runs between Morne Puilboreau and Morne Haleine. To some extent one must conclude that the orientation of this area is an advantage as well as its soils, for on south-facing slopes with youthful andesite soils the main crops are rice, corn, and plantains rather than coffee.

Distinctly poorer than all the other soils of the region are the lateritic soils developed on andesite; consequently they are used mainly for the less demanding crops. Guinea grass, manioc, and beans occupy most of the steeper slopes, while in the valleys, where drainage is less excessive, rice occupies much of the land. In addition, on the last-named sites a good deal of coffee is also grown. Although in general the fertility of the soil is low, the fact that it is deep, well drained, slightly acid, and has a high potassium content makes it reasonably suitable for coffee.

Two physiographic divisions within the region remain to be discussed. The less important is the ash-covered extinct volcano, Morne Mapoux. Here the main problem facing agriculture is not soil fertility, though drainage is excessive and much leaching has occurred. A greater handicap is the rapid gullying which is taking place. Slopes are very steep, and the whole mountain top is scarred by minor landslides. Rice, manioc and corn are grown, but only about 30 per cent of the land is in cultivation.

The last area to be dealt with, but one of the most productive, is the flood plain of the Trois Rivières. Interrupted here and there by rock ridges which cross the valley from north to south, the plain is divided into several sections all of which have loamy soils developed on sand. Forunately, the Trois Rivières is quite well entrenched within its valley and so widespread flooding is relatively rare. The short but hard rains of thunderstorms seldom cause the stream to overflow its banks, and even prolonged hurricane rains rarely inundate the plain to depths exceeding two or three feet. Floods are therefore sufficiently frequent to help enrich the soil but not so serious as to pose a major hazard for agriculture. In consequence the entire plain is intensively used. Coffee, plaintains, rice, and corn are the main crops, though near Pilate a small section which receives relatively little rain produces sugar cane, corn, and plantains, instead of the crop combination which is more generally used.

Population distribution in the region, though generally dense, shows significant correlations with soil productivity, relief, and the danger of flooding. On the broadest scale, one notes a distinctly larger number of dwellings per square mile in the more humid southwestern part of the valley than in the less humid northeast. At a lower level of generalization densities are seen to be smaller in the hilly parts of the valley than in areas of low relief. Particularly large numbers of houses are built in and around the flood plain, where the gentlest slopes and the highest productivity are to be found; clearly the advantages of living near the river generally outweigh the disadvantages of occasional floods. The author observed waterlines on house walls nearly as high as the window sills and was told of buildings and people being washed away by the stream when in spate. Nevertheless, in the various sections of the flood plain, houses are found everywhere except in the downstream extremities where inundations are most frequent.

The areas with lateritic soils, suffering both from high relief and low productivity, are very sparsely peopled. The only significant clusters of houses are in the coffee groves.

Minor influences on the location of houses are the steepness of the slopes and the availability of water. Valleys are the preferred sites for dwellings throughout the shale and andesite areas, though ridge tops are not infrequently used. The ridges and valleys, however, are so small and so close together that their influence over house location is scarcely evident in a generalized population map such as Figure 19.

Citadelle Humid Interior Limestone Hills

The bulk of this region is made up of massive limestone ridges, upon which the soil covering is rather variable in depth. Quite extensive areas have fairly deep clay loam soil, well drained and well endowed with plant nutrients, particularly potassium. Most of this soil is planted in coffee, a crop for which it is well suited. In addition, near the eastern margin of the region, where the wet season lasts only six or seven months, plantains are often found with the coffee. Throughout most of the region, however, the deep limestone soils are in coffee alone or coffee with taro.

The reason for the nearly exclusive use of the deep soils for coffee is that adequate amounts of most other food products may be derived from the extensive areas of shallow limestone soils, which are very fertile. Here, despite the large amount of rock at the surface, most of the land is quite intensively used. Plant nutrients and moisture are sufficient to produce good yields of corn, plantains, and sweet potatoes as well as of the less demanding manioc, beans, and sugar cane. Almost half the land is in crops at any one time. The main time for planting is April and May, just at the beginning of the wet season. Plantains, however, may be started at any time from January to September and sweet potatoes in any month of the year. Consequently seasonal food shortages are rare or unknown.

In only a few small areas is the soil cover on the limestone so thin that it cannot produce any crops. These areas have a vegetation of broadleaf trees, which grow by thrusting their roots into fissures in the rock. The only section of this type large enough to be mapped is the crest of the ridge upon which the Citadelle has been constructed. The boundary of this area around the fortress has been drawn to include some potentially productive land in which agriculture is prohibited by law.

Although the region is essentially one of limestone hills, it contains deep valleys, eroded, in strata of shale, by the Rivière Bouyaha and its tributaries. These valleys stand out as the sections of most intensive land utilization (Plate 5). Their residual soils are fine-textured and easily retain their moisture throughout the year, while even the alluvium is fine sand or silt upon which there has developed a heavy-textured soil which resists desiccation in dry weather. Consequently a rich and varied agriculture is possible, and the land has the appearance of great prosperity.

The specific associations between crops and soils in the valleys of the region are similar to those of the Plaisance Garden. Soils developed on shale, because of their imperfect drainage, are devoted largely to rice, though much corn is grown as well, and the best sites are in coffee. The flood plains, which are only rarely inundated, are devoted principally to coffee and plantains, though in areas of finest texture rice is grown instead. In the extreme south, where the dry season becomes more pronounced, corn and sugar cane are important flood-plain crops.

Included for convenience within the western portion of the Citadelle Humid Interior Limestone Hills, but more typical of other regions, are two hills of andesite and one of quartz diorite. The former are largely in corn and beans with a few coffee groves and are similar to andesitic sections of the Bedoret Humid Volcanic Hills. The latter, like sections of the Lafleur Humid Quartz Diorite Hills, contains some corn, manioc, and rice, but is mainly in broadleaf forest.

Population distribution in the region is closely correlated with relief, with most of the people living in the valleys. Valley sites are preferred, not only for their greater productivity, but also because of the availability of level land for house sites and the ease of access to water supplies. Fortunately, only a narrow strip of land along the Bouyaha River is so frequently flooded that it is avoided by home-builders.

It is evident that many of the inhabitants of the valley work in the hills during at least part of the year. Yet the hills also contain a considerable number of dwellings. The rock here is less jagged than in the Brigand Coastal Hills so that travel is easier and suitable house sites are more numerous. Only the slopes of the steepest ridges are completely uninhabited, and in the areas of deep limestone hills soils, especially in the eastern and western extremities of the region, the population densities may rival those of the valleys.

Bahon Subhumid Quartz Diorite Hills
This region comprises those portions of the crystalline core of the Massif du Nord in which agricultural land use clearly dominates in the landscape (Plate 6).

Geologically the region is homogeneous, being almost completely underlain by quartz diorite. Climatically it is not quite so uniform, but for the most part it is neither so humid that its soils are excessively leached, nor so deficient in moisture as seriously to handicap agriculture. Six to eight months of the year are classed as wet and only one or two months are dry. The overburden, furthermore, is deep enough and the surface soils sufficiently heavy-textured to remain relatively moist throughout this dry period. Consequently the land is more useful for farming than its rather unimpressive fertility would suggest. It is almost all cultivated periodically, though a rest period of about four years must be provided after two years of cultivation, and, therefore, only about 30 per cent of the total area is under production at any one time.

The leading crops on the hill slopes are corn, manioc, rice, and beans. The corn, being the most demanding, is grown mainly on freshly rested land, and often in association with manioc, planting taking place usually in April or May just before the first rains. Rice and beans are also planted together, the former being started in July, after the soil moisture has been replenished by the rains of May and June, but before the longer rainy period in late summer and fall. When the rice has sprouted, beans are commonly planted in the same fields and reach maturity some time after the rice has been harvested. On some north-facing slopes there are also small groves of coffee.

Although yields within the region are never high, the variety of crops grown and the staggering of the planting season help reduce the hazard of occasional droughts. If one type of plant does not yield a harvest, another usually does. Complete crop failures are virtually unknown.

A greater agricultural handicap than drought on most steep sites is gully erosion. In no other type of bedrock within the Département is dissection as intricate as in quartz diorite, and there is no doubt that this dissection has been accelerated by the clearing of land for agriculture. Probably one-quarter to one-third of the fields have been damaged by gullies.

The areas with most severe gullying, however, are not the hill slopes with youthful soils but rather the rainy crests of the northern ridge of the Massif where deep lateritic soils have developed. Here soil fertility is low in any case, and many sections have been so deeply eroded as to be of little value for farming. Some rice, beans, and manioc are grown, but most land of this type is in short grasses or low shrubs and trees.

Within the uplands there are also areas of lower relief. These are all stream-cut basins, most of which, unfortunately, are being redissected by tributaries of the pirate Grande Rivière. Gradients are, however, still gentler than in surrounding hills and soils are deeper and richer. Agriculture is consequently on a somewhat higher level of intensity. Nearly half of the land is farmed at any one time, much of it being in plantains and coffee, though manioc and other crops of the steeper slopes are grown as well.

Plantains and coffee also occupy the floor of the Grande Rivière valley below Bahon. As this stream is continually expanding its drainage area by headwater capture, its lower section exhibits many characteristics of rejuvenation, such as the incision of its present channel ten to fifteen feet within the flood plain in the section between the towns of Bahon and Grande Rivière. The alluvium of the plain is therefore very well drained, high enough to escape flooding, and suitable for intensive farming.

Population distribution in the region, in its broad pattern, is related directly to the productivity of the land. For example, as rainfall declines from north to south, so does the population density. In addition, productive valleys, such as that of the Grande Rivière, are occupied by dense concentrations of people. The only notable exception to this generalization is found in parts of the region adjacent to humid sections of the Plaine du Nord; here the hills are cultivated by farmers who live in the plain.

Terrain does have some effect on house location, but as the hill slopes are not as smooth as in regions of volcanic rock house sites are fairly abundant. Ridge tops need not be utilized and most of them are unoccupied, dwellings being constructed preferably on the slopes, particularly on lower slopes, close to the water supply provided by streams. Fortunately streams are so numerous in the region that adherence to this locative principle does not result in any excessive separation of house from farm.

Vallière Sparsely Populated Hills

This region contains a variety of different types of rocks and soils, yet it is unified by the fact that most of the land is suitable for agriculture only on a very limited scale. Although six or seven months of the year are wet, three or four are dry, and only on the most favoured sites is more than a quarter of the land in harvested crops.

The poorest soils are those developed on granite, not merely because of their low fertility, but because they are coarse-textured and become desiccated during the dry season. Originally, most of the granite areas were covered with tropical yellow pines, and these trees are still to be found throughout the region except on a few humid windward sites occupied by broadleaf species. Today, however, extensive dense coniferous stands are only found in places where, for reasons of inaccessibility or extremely poor soil, agriculture has not yet been attempted. The greater part of the pine forest has suffered the inroads of peasant farmers. Here and there one sees beans, manioc, and other food crops growing in scattered clearings, and more commonly one is confronted with evidence that farming has been initiated and then abandoned. In large tracts, huge pines, up to eighty feet tall and two feet in diameter, are dispersed over a landscape where the ground cover consists of a dense growth of coarse grasses, but where no young pine seedlings are to be seen (Plate 17). In these glades little or no regeneration of the pines is taking place. It is clear, therefore, that in the not too distant future the land may well revert entirely to grasses. It is equally clear that prevailing agricultural practices are largely responsible for the change. Prior to cultivation, the land is cleared by fire, which destroys all low growth, sears mature trees to heights of fifty feet above the ground, and often kills them also. Even a relatively infrequent repetition of this procedure can reduce the density of surviving trees below the critical level needful for recolonization. It is in fact possible that in some areas a single burning will effect the destruction of the forest. Taking into consideration the percentage of land now under cultivation in the granite, and the relatively short history of occupancy in the area, one may safely assume that few tracts have been burned and farmed more than two or three times, yet the results of this activity are alarmingly enduring.

Another portion of the granite area has grasses and coniferous trees as a natural cover, and not one which has been produced as a result of human activity. This section is near the southern boundary of the region in an area where rainfall is so deficient that pines can survive only on the northern flanks of hills, while south-facing slopes remain in grass. Here one finds a patchwork of dense, self-sustaining coniferous stands alternating with open grassland. Unfortunately, the pattern is on too small a scale to be clearly depicted on the land use map.

In both open and dense pine forests, sporadic cutting of trees for fuel has been going on for a long time. The high resin content of the wood makes it particularly useful for kindling, and as such it finds its way into almost every market of the Département. Because of this very resin, however, the wood is extremely difficult to saw by hand, and the extraction of lumber on a commercial scale dates only from about 1948. Since that date about half a dozen small saw mills have been established at the termini of private roads built into the pine forests from Cerca la Source, Lamielle, and La Victoire. No attempt to conserve existing stands and no replanting appear to have taken place. Each mill has been moved, on the average, once every two years, and only the most inaccessible of the good stands remain untouched. It is not likely that sustained timber yields on a scale any greater than the present modest rate of exploitation will be possible under existing methods of production.

Areas of shale are more extensive but scarcely more productive than those underlain by granite, even though much of the soil which originally developed on the shale was deeper and more fertile than the soil formed on granite. Indeed, in the northern and central parts of the region, under some existing stands of virgin pine the shale is still clothed with a layer of fairly fertile, stone-free residual silt loam, one to three feet in depth, which appears to have agricultural possibilities. Yet the exploitation of these possibilities has had unfortunate results, for deforestation of the shale is commonly followed by sheet erosion which removes this fine-textured material more rapidly than it is replaced through weathering of the bedrock. Newly cleared land is used fairly intensively for corn, plantains, beans, sweet potatoes, and other fairly demanding crops, but within a relatively short period the soil tends to wash away leaving only an incomplete cover of rock fragments in a layer five or six inches thick. Even this poor seedbed is able for a time to give low yields of a variety of crops, thanks to its content of nitrates and phosphorus, but long periods of rest under guinea grass are necessary between plantings. Eventually it too may go, and the rocky slope which remains is barely able to maintain a cover of coarse grasses and scattered pines.

This rapid deterioration of the solum is most pronounced on south-facing slopes, which are relatively hot and dry. Where slopes are to the north, the soil may be considerably more durable, and may support regular cultivation, as noted, for example, in the case of some long ridges near Bois Laurence. These ridges are oriented at right angles to the winter onshore winds and are also closer to the Atlantic than other shale hills within the region. Consequently they are somewhat more humid and, under the greater humidity, the bedrock breaks down more rapidly. Although these slopes are completely cleared, they retain six to ten inches of rather stony silt loam overburden, enough to permit the cultivation of corn, beans, manioc, plantains, and other crops, though a long rest period under guinea grass is necessary.

In the southern part of the region, where the moisture deficiency is greater, shale slopes, even if they have never been cultivated, are covered by only three to six inches of overburden, and the peasants realize that the land should not be cleared. The vegetation consists of pines and grasses, and, as in the granite, it is possible to distinguish between these areas, which were never suitable for agriculture, and the sections to the north which have been ruined by cultivation. In the latter, the pines are distributed irregularly, regardless of exposure. In the former, tree growth is restricted to north-facing slopes, and stands of rather dense coniferous forest alternate with stretches of open grassland.

More productive generally than the areas of shale are those of quartz diorite. The reason is not that the original soil was more fertile or more moisture retentive, but that it is less sensitive to rough treatment. The abundant quartz crystals in the quartz diorite soils help retard sheet erosion, so that, although gullies develop, most slopes retain some overburden. The soil, it is true, may be very poor. It may require eight to ten years of rest after only two years in crops. Yet after lying idle for that length of time, most areas of quartz diorite seem capable of producing a harvest of some kind. As a result one does not see large abandoned stretches, too poor to be farmed again in the present generation. Instead there is evidence of a long-term land rotation in which most areas are periodically cultivated. Rice, manioc, and beans are the leading crops, occupying about 10 per cent of the land on the steepest slopes and no more than 35 per cent on sites with gentle gradients. Unforunately, the repeated clearing of the land by fire has destroyed almost all vestiges of the pine forests which were once even more luxuriant on the quartz diorite than on the granite and shale. Here and there a few small stands of pines remain, but the most common vegetation is semideciduous scrub which springs up after the land has been taken out of cultivation.

The best residual soils in the region, from the point of view of agriculture, are to be found in the andesitic hills of the extreme southeast. The durability of these soils, or rather the rate at which they are renewed through weathering of the bedrock, is indeed remarkable. Even cleared slopes with measured gradients of 100 per cent were found to possess a foot of fertile, fairly fine-textured overburden. In these virtually indestructable soils, even under rather stringent climatic conditions, harvests may be secured. All north-facing slopes of andesite are cleared and occupied, and much the same crop association is found as in the more humid andesitic areas to the northwest. Corn, beans, plantains, manioc, and rice are major crops, while the land is periodically rested for two or three years under guinea grass.

On the south-facing slopes of these hills, however, the climate is Type VI or Type VII and the dry season is so severe that even andesite soils are not productive. The overburden drops to about six inches in depth and intensive farming is no longer possible. Some corn, millet, beans, and plantains are found in troughs, but the slopes are mainly clothed with pines and grasses.

Of equal value with the best andesite soils are the soils of the alluvial terraces. Found in association with several streams near the village of Bois Laurence, these stretches of fine sand are almost entirely given over to agriculture. Corn is the leading crop, but rice, beans, and plantains are also widely grown, as well as a little coffee. The amount of moisture absorbed during the rainy weather in this permeable land of low relief is evidently sufficient for most quick-growing crops and will enable some perennial plants to survive the dry season.

Unfortunately, the stream terraces and humid andesite slopes occupy very limited areas. The region as a whole, therefore, produces a relatively small amount of food. Production is also highly seasonal. Normally planting is only possible between May and August, and only one harvest is obtained annually. During the long interval when the ground yields little or nothing, the farmers must depend largely on stored rice, corn, and beans, but in few cases can an individual set up enough to provide an adequate food supply from one harvest to the next. In comparison with other more richly endowed parts of the Département, this region is, therefore, rather sparsely settled. Fairly high population densities are found only in a few freshly cleared shale areas, where the soils have not yet been ruined, and on the productive andesite slopes and stream terraces. The drier shale areas and large tracts of granite are virtually uninhabited.

Since there is little or no competition for house sites, and since each household operates over a wide area, it is feasible to locate most dwellings near streams. Only in the andesite, and to some extent in the quartz diorite, are people so attached to limited landholdings that they build their homes on the ridges.

Carice Lateritic Plateau

This broad stream-cut basin, formed mainly in quartz diorite rock, drains towards the south but is not separated by any mountain barrier from the Atlantic. It therefore receives a considerable amount of winter rain and the dry season is only one or two months long. Slopes are gentle, drainage is generally good, and the deep red soils which originally developed still largely remain despite a century or more of cultivation.

Nevertheless, the soils are of low fertility, and consequently of limited agricultural value. This limitation is most evident on convex sites, especially in the northeastern parts of the region, where the soils are the deepest and the most mature, but most heavily leached, especially of their phosphorus and potassium. Here, despite the favourable rainfall regime, the only crops that seem to thrive are the tolerant manioc, rice, and beans, though some corn, plantains, and sweet potatoes are also grown. Between periods of cropping the land must be rested so long that many idle fields have a covering of shrubs eight to ten feet tall, and only about one-third of the land is in use at any one time. Some young coffee was observed, set out in tracts freshly cleared of scrub, but, in the absence of fertilizer, satisfactory yields are unlikely.

The only area of deep lateritic soil in the region which has been demonstrated to be suitable for coffee is found around Mont Organisé, where the bedrock is andesite. Even here, however, the area in coffee is small, and most of the land supports a crop association identical to that found in the quartz diorite. That the vast difference in the amount of plant nutrients originally contained in the two rock types is not more evident in the land use pattern is an indication of the dominance here of climate over bedrock as the main edaphic determinant.

On depressional sites and in the southwestern part of the region, because of impeded drainage or lower precipitation, the soil is generally more youthful, less leached, and more productive than in the area discussed above. Fertility is still not high, as is seen in the continued presence of manioc and rice as the major crops and in the absence of plantains. The chemical characteristics of the soil, however, meet the specific requirements of coffee, which is cultivated on a large scale. About half of the land is under crops at any one time, a proportion which reflects the conservational character of coffee culture as practised in the Département, and should not be taken as an indication that this soil would be quickly regenerated after a period in general food crops.

This region also contains, eroded within the quartz diorite, some depressions which are so level and poorly drained that they have a covering of organic matter up to a foot or more in depth. These peat bogs are unique within the Département and support no vegetation other than grasses about two feet tall. If the layer of organic matter were removed or fertilized, the bogs might be used for rice production, but as they stand, the surface material is evidently too deficient in plant nutrients to support any type of cultivation.

Although the greater part of the region is one of deep residual soils, it also contains strips of alluvium which are, in fact, its most productive sections. The alluvium is associated with the Rivière Ténèbres and its tributaries, and is found not only on the existing flood plain but also on terraces marking the former levels of this rejuvenated stream. The highest terraces are mainly sandy, while lower ones, including the most recently formed flood plain, are silty in texture. These areas are not all of equal value, for the sand is of limited fertility, rather excessively drained, and used mainly for rice, manioc, beans, and coffee, a crop association similar to that found in most youthful lateritic soils. The areas of silt, however, rival in productivity the best land of the Plaisance Garden. The silt soil is sufficiently fertile for the most demanding plants, and sufficiently moisture retentive to permit crops to grow well throughout the year. Consequently, the lower terraces and the flood plain are cultivated continuously and almost completely, the main crops being corn and rice, commonly planted together, and coffee. Plantains are not plentiful, evidently because of the imperfect drainage.

Planting, here and throughout most of the region, is carried out from April to July, just before or at the beginning of the rainy season, and the main harvest comes in November and December. In the northeast, however, around Mont Organisé, more precipitation is received during the winter months, and both the planting and harvesting seasons are about two months longer than elsewhere in the region. Consequently, food production is spread out fairly well throughout the year. Considerable surpluses are on hand during the main harvest period, and supplies remain reasonably adequate throughout the remainder of the year.

Included within the region are one isolated hill and a few low ridges of quartz diorite where, because of the steep slopes, the soils are shallow. These areas are similar to sections of the Bahon Subhumid Quartz Diorite Hills and the Vallière Sparsely Populated Hills in that the main crops on more humid sites are manioc, rice, and corn, while drier areas are used for manioc, rice, and beans. A third or less of the land is in simultaneous cultivation.

The population distribution in the region is quite even. Only the most poorly drained sections and the hilly areas with shallow soils are not used for house sites. Elsewhere there are few physical restrictions on the locations of dwellings, and people tend to build their homes on the land they cultivate. Because of their greater productivity, the areas of youthful lateritic soils and the areas of alluvium are somewhat more densely settled than other parts of the region.

Ranquitte Basin and Adjacent Hills

This region is essentially an area of shale bedrock with sufficient precipitation during the wet season of six to seven months to permit a fairly complete, though not a very intensive, agricultural use of the land.

Most of the land is steeply sloping. Stretching from north of Ranquitte to the eastern boundary of the region is a range of hills with gradients averaging about 50 per cent, while even steeper slopes, of the order of 100 per cent, are found in the gorges cut into the basin floor by tributaries of the Grande Rivière. On all these slopes the overburden is quite shallow, consisting mainly of small particles, of the size of coarse sand, weathered from the bedrock. The depth of the loose material is generally less than six inches on the hills and about half that on the sides of the gorges.

Fortunately, although the overburden is thin, it is not becoming thinner. Under the moisture conditions prevailing here, the disintegration of the shale produces enough new unconsolidated material to replace the amount lost through erosion, provided that the land is permitted to grow up in shrubs for a period of three or four years after each year or two of cultivation. The peasants are always careful to preserve some overburden on the rock.

Though shallow and coarse, the surface material is sufficiently endowed with plant nutrients to support some farming. Chemically it is not unsuited to corn, which is the major crop, while beans and some manioc are also produced. The greatest problem is desiccation of the soil in the dry season, due to its poor capacity for moisture-retention. The corn and beans cannot be planted before May or June and are harvested in September or October, before the really dry period sets in. Manioc is planted later, in July and August, and is almost the only crop capable of surviving the winter. Because of the rest period required, only 20 to 40 per cent of the land is under cultivation at any one time.

The only steep slopes on which more intensive farming is possible are within a few valleys on the relatively humid northeastern side of the ridge north of Ranquitte. Here the soils are somewhat deeper than those described above and many small coffee groves are to be found. The presence of these patches of perennial agriculture raises the percentage of land under crops to about 50 per cent.

The region also contains some less steeply sloping sections. Of these, the largest are remnants of the plain carved by south-flowing streams before the piracy of the Grande Rivière, while smaller areas with gentle slopes are found in a few basins cut into zones of relatively soft rock near Mombin Crochu.

Little, if any, of this land is now truly level. Most areas are lightly dissected, with slopes of the order of 10 to 20 per cent. Yet erosion is sufficiently slow to permit the retention of a layer of overburden which is usually ten to twenty inches in depth, with a surface soil of stone-free silt loam. On this soil, agriculture is relatively rich and varied.

Corn is still the dominant crop, because it is best able to benefit by the high potassium content and the slight acidity of the soil. Beans and manioc are also found, mainly on ridges, while depressions are devoted largely to coffee and plantains. The superiority of this land is seen not only in the type of crops grown, but also in the intensity of exploitation. Over 60 per cent of the total area is cultivated simultaneously, and enough food is usually produced to last through the year, though by March and April supplies tend to become rather depleted.

Somewhat different from the remainder of the region is the crest of the range of hills north of Ranquitte. The bedrock here is a rather soft limestone. The overburden, though fairly continuous, is shallow, and, due to the permeability of the bedrock, even more droughty than the overburden on shale. Consequently, though some manioc and beans are grown, most of the land is in grasses or shrubs with scattered pine trees.

The distribution of dwellings within the region reflects its almost perfect inverse correlation between slope and productivity. Most of the houses are located on the terraces and in the basins, where construction is easy and farming is most rewarding. The hills are very sparsely populated and, where surrounded by areas of low relief, may be entirely uninhabited.

A secondary factor governing the location of dwellings, operative only in the eastern part of the region, is the availability of water. Through this area flow several permanent streams, not greatly incised below the general level of the land, and dwellings tend to be concentrated along their banks. To the west, however, the only permanent streams form part of the Grande Rivière system and lie at the bottom of deep, entirely uninhabitable, V-shaped gorges. In this section of the region all the houses are on the upper terraces, where interfluves, rather than valleys, are the preferred sites. The benefits of good drainage are evidently more important than close proximity to a seasonal source of water, and, in any case, streams are so numerous and so evenly spaced on the terraces that any house site is fairly close to one or more of them.

Cerca la Source Savanna
The most distinctive characteristic of this region is its lack of moisture.

The dry season is one of intense drought, recording less than an inch of rain over a period of three to five months. And though four to six months are classed as wet, the greater part of the region has no over-burden to absorb the moisture. Gradients are generally from 30 to 50 per cent, and under the prevailing climatic conditions weathered material is stripped from the slopes more rapidly than it is replaced by disintegration of the shale bedrock. Consequently, a large dissected section of the basin floor and most of the hilly country to the north comprises a vast outcropping of steeply dipping rock beds. Upon this surface, rain water does not remain, but rushes away in intermittent watercourses, which here form a network more intricate than in any other part of the Département (Plate 7).

These areas without overburden are not devoid of vegetation. Hillsides are generally covered with grasses, growing in fissures in the rock, while some north-facing slopes even support a few pine trees. The drier, dissected basin floor has a vegetation consisting mainly of xerophytic scrub.

Somewhat better conditions exist along the valley bottoms, where small ribbons of sand have been deposited here and there. Although most of the streams in the area are youthful, variations in the hardness of the bedrock cause some sections to erode more quickly than others, and in the zones of relatively soft rock many of the streams assume, for short distances, some characteristics of maturity. The narrow flood plains they have laid down represent the only areas in which cultivation is possible in this part of the region. Millet, corn, beans, manioc, and sisal are grown: the first three are able to reach maturity during the short rainy period, while the last two manage to survive the dry weather. Planting is carried out mainly betwen April and June, though beans are sometimes successfully started as late as August. In many years, however, there are almost complete crop failures.

In order to obtain cash with which to purchase food from other areas, the people of this district specialize in certain handicrafts. Baskets are woven, and, in the absence of a factory to process sisal, this fibre is extracted by hand and made into bags and ropes. A somewhat larger source of income is provided by the sale of livestock, which are grazed on the rocky slopes. Cattle are most important, followed, in order, by horses, goats, donkeys, and chickens. Yet total earnings are inadequate to prevent the occurrence of periods of want and hunger. The trade of the area, so important to the peasants, is nevertheless so limited in its actual value and volume that no commercial trucks find it profitable to travel even to Saltadère, the only village of the area, and one which is located on a fairly good road. The only modern transport which uses the road regularly consists of military vehicles and trucks carrying boards from the saw mills at Lamielle.

One attempt on the part of the government to assist these people has been the establishment at Saltadère of an experimental lime orchard. The trees are not doing badly, but no market for the fruit has been established, and none of the peasants have taken up lime-growing. An irrigation project was started but abandoned.

Fortunately, the dissected shale plain and hills do not constitute the whole of the region. Included within it are two areas of greater productivity, of which the less important is the northern slope of the limestone ridge which here froms the southern boundary of the Département. The slope is steep and possesses only thin, scattered pockets of soil, but the soil is moisture-retentive, and the ridge intercepts enough rainfall to permit the growth of broadleaf trees thirty to forty feet high. These trees still remain to form a forest cover of moderate density on the highest, most precipitous part of the ridge. Lower slopes are used to produce guinea grass, manioc, corn, sweet potatoes, and plantains, though only about one-third of the land is cultivated at any one time.

The second productive zone, and by far the best farming area in the region, comprises the former flood plain of the Rivière Océan (Plate 7). Formed along the base of the limestone escarpment, this plain is about ten miles long, and up to a mile in width. Because of its rejuvenation, the stream is now incised some forty feet into the plain, but, except in the extreme east, the plain itself has not been greatly dissected. Considerable sheet erosion has, however, occurred with the result that most fine alluvium has been stripped away. Terraces adjacent to the river consist mainly of coarse sand and gravel, while, farther from the stream, the plain is floored by shale or by marl derived from the limestone to the south.

The shale sections of this plain are much more useful than shale areas elsewhere in the region. Because of the less rapid run-off and less severe erosion here, the regolith has, in most places, attained a depth of a foot or two, and has developed a sandy loam surface soil. Fertility is quite high, and, where the overburden is more than eighteen inches in depth, corn and sugar cane are quite intensively grown, about three-quarters of the land being in simultaneous cultivation. A similar land use pattern is found in those areas which are fairly fine-textured as well as in the deep heavy marlaceous soils, which are the most drought-resistant in the region.

On the other hand, the shallower shale soils and the coarse gravels tend to dry out rather completely during the winter, and are used principally for corn, manioc, and beans. In soils of the former type about one-third of the land is in use at any one time, while in the latter the proportion drops to about half that amount.

One small irrigated area is found on the southern side of the Océan plain, roughly midway between Cerca la Source and Saltadère. Here a stream issues from the face of the escarpment, providing enough water to permit heavy and sustained production of rice, plantains, sugar cane, corn, and other crops on about three hundred acres of marl soils.

The settlement pattern in the region, as might be expected, shows a marked concentration of population on the Océan plain. In addition to its productivity, this area is easy to build on, free from flooding, and near a permanent water supply. Nevertheless, the dissected shale area is occupied by a considerable number of people. Located near the strips of arable land, their huts are built on low ridges, which offer ease of construction and freedom from flooding, but no convenient source of water. During much of the year, the small streams of this area are dry, and water supplies must be transported, in some cases for several miles, from the Artibonite and Océan rivers.

The area with the lowest population in the region is the limestone escarpment. Farmed by people who live in the plains below, the escarpment zone contains virtually no dwellings at all.

Pignon Plain and Adjacent Hills

This region is no more humid than the Cerca la Source Basin, but because of its generally lower relief it has deeper soils and is far more productive.

The core of the region is a plain comprising the most northerly section of the Central Plateau. Still largely undissected, the plain is relatively uniform in relief and also in the length and severity of its dry season; the period from December to March is almost rainless. During the remainder of the year, precipitation is generally moderate but is not quite evenly distributed; more falls east of Pignon than to the west and southwest. Nevertheless, in determining the land use pattern throughout the region, the variations of climate are less directly significant than those of land type and soil.

East of Pignon the most extensive land types are alluvial sand and gravel terraces. Rather excessively drained, the terraces are too droughty for forest, but are capable of supporting a complete cover of grasses and are therefore suitable for grazing. This area is unique in the Département in that grazing land is held in common and livestock are permitted to run free (Plate 8 and 20). The most important animals are cattle and horses, though goats, pigs, and a few sheep are also raised. In quality, they tend to be rather low; cattle often give no milk before they are four or five years old. Nevertheless, the sale of livestock provides the main cash income for the people here.

Although pastoral activities dominate in this area, it also contains a substantial number of gardens. To keep out the livestock, all these cultivated tracts are surrounded by fences formed of slim poles planted close together and linked one to another by vines. If an animal manages to force his way into a garden, no liability is attached to his owner; rather the proprietor of the garden is at fault for not having made his fence sufficiently strong! These fenced gardens produce a large part of the food required locally. Corn is the leading crop, planted in May and ripening before the rains cease. Beans and some rice, planted as late as June or July, are often able to reach maturity before the dry season sets in. In addition some manioc and sugar cane are planted, but as these crops must survive at least one dry season before they come into production, the time of planting is less critical. All that is necessary is that the root systems be well established before the dry weather starts, and these crops are started in any month between May and August. About half of the land in each enclosure is in cultivation at any one time, the remainder being allowed to rest.

The area thus produces a variety of agricultural commodities. Nevertheless, there is seldom any surplus of food for sale, and some provisions must be purchased. Plantains, specifically, are bought whenever possible, as this favourite food cannot be produced here without irrigation.

As indicated above, the combination of open range and fenced fields has developed in response particularly to the productive capacity of alluvial terraces. Nevertheless, the system has been extended to some extent into inliers and salients of better land, including the valley of the Rivière Guape, where the high water table is a major agricultural asset, and some areas with deep, heavy, drought-resistant marlaceous and limestone plain soils. In the Guape Valley, however, the fenced fields are devoted almost entirely to corn, while on the marl and limestone plains sugar cane occupies nearly half of the cultivated land. Also, in these areas well suited to agriculture, almost 80 per cent of the land is enclosed as compared with about 40 per cent in much of the sand plain and less than 10 per cent in the gravel.

The drier part of the plain south of Pignon is almost useless agriculturally. Where soils are coarse-textured, as in gravel terraces, the land is almost devoid of vegetation, and even in the rainy season supports only scattered clumps of thorn bushes and coarse bunch grasses. Where limestone plains are found, near the southern boundary of the region, the rock is covered, not by two or three feet of overburden as is the case east of Pignon, but by only two or three inches of fine loam. This thin layer of earth, with its vegetation of short grasses, becomes, of course, completely desiccated during the dry season. Neither land type can produce crops, and neither provides forage except for a few emaciated sheep and goats.

The remaining part of this drier section of the plain comprises about half of the total area of the region and is located, in the main, to the west of Pignon. Here, upon bedrock consisting largely of limestone and marl, the soils are fertile and fairly heavy-textured, but very variable in thickness. Over the limestone, the depth of the loose material ranges from an inch or two to several feet. Soil developed on marl tends to be consistently deeper, but usually contains a calcareous hardpan not far from the surface.

In this area, the use made of the land depends largely on the depth of the soil. Where the depth is less than three inches over limestone or hardpan, cultivation does not occur, and the ground cover consists of open forest and scrub. The trees are now used principally as a source of firewood. Mahogany, which was once fairly plentiful and was used for timber, has been almost all cut out.

With the limestone or hardpan three to six inches below the surface, agriculture is possible, and corn and sugar cane are the main crops. The former produces a quick harvest which can be used immediately or stored for consumption during the dry season. The sugar cane, for which the soil is well suited, is processed locally into rum or molasses for cash sale. However, a year or two in crops exhausts the fertility of the land, and it must then be rested for two or three years.

Sugar cane and corn are also the leading crops in areas with more than six inches of soil over the limestone or hardpan, but here yields are higher than in areas with shallower soil and little if any rest period is required for the land. Over 70 per cent of the total area is in crops during the rainy season. Nevertheless, even this area is not self-sufficient in food and traditionally suffers periodic shortages despite the cash income derived from cane products.

A major benefit introduced into this area has been the construction, by the Service Coöperatif Interamericain de Production Agricole (SCIPA), of an irrigation canal ten miles in length on the west side of the Rivière Bouyaha. Through this canal, water from the Bouyaha is at present supplied to some 3,000 acres of land. The Bouyaha is a stream eminently well suited to this use, for its headwaters are in humid uplands to the north, and most of its course above St. Raphaël is in limestone. In this type of rock the river passes through a long succession of deep pools which act as reservoirs controlling the flow of water, and keeping the river fairly free of silt. The lowest monthly flow of the Bouyaha, according to the SCIPA records, is 1.5 m³/sec., in January, a figure which is nearly one-quarter of its maximum flow of 5.7 m³/sec. in May and November. There is therefore a fairly reliable supply of clear water entering the canal at its start, above St. Raphaël, where a small dam has been built to effect the diversion.

The irrigated land is indeed an oasis of year-round productivity which is not only a delight to look upon, but a salvation to the people in times of drought. Rice, corn, and plantains are the main crops at present, though some tobacco is also being produced on an experimental farm and on peasant plots.

Over-all plans for this project involve the ultimate irrigation of 6,000 acres, though it is recognized that the amount of water available, even supplemented by rainfall, will fall short of providing the optimum supply. The deficiency is estimated to be about 40 per cent in March and April and 15 to 30 per cent in most other months except November and December, when supply, for a brief period, catches up with demand. However, a detailed planting timetable has been worked out whereby the less demanding crops, such as tobacco and sweet potatoes, will be grown during the period of greatest moisture deficiency, while, at other times in the year, more exacting plants such as vegetables and rice will occupy the land. It has been possible in this way to schedule a harvest of some kind every month or two throughout the year.

The full effectuation of this scheme, however, faces several obstacles. One is a physical problem in that the irrigation canal, in its course along the contour, crosses an area of permeable limestone where serious leakages have developed. Other difficulties are human. Although SCIPA constructed the canal using its own resources and provides water free for the peasants, it has no control over the land itself. The planting schedule is entirely an advisory one, and may or may not be followed. Also, desilting of the canal, which is essential from time to time, is the responsibility of those who benefit by it, yet no legal machinery exists to compel them to do the work. On this point a good deal of friction has developed, and the canal has deteriorated considerably since its construction in 1953.

Despite these difficulties, from every point of view except possibly the financial one, the project may be considered highly successful. It is unfortunate that the Bouyaha has not enough water to permit a similar scheme on the east bank of the river, where the soils are generally deeper and more useful than to the west.

In the extreme south of the region, the overlying marl and alluvium have been stripped away to expose an area of Miocene conglomerate. Here the surface materials are quite coarse, but are unconsolidated to a depth sufficient to absorb a fair amount of water in the wet season. Furthermore, since the rock becomes very compact a few feet from the surface, this moisture is not able to escape downwards beyond the reach of plant roots. It is therefore possible to raise such crops as corn, manioc, and beans. Yields are low and uncertain, however, and only about one-third of the land is in cultivation at any one time.

Last to be discussed of the physiographic units in the western section of the plain, but the most productive under natural conditions is the flood plain of the Rivière Bouyaha. Agriculturally this area is similar to flood plains in the northern part of the Département and is intensively used for the production of corn and plantains. Unfortunately the plain is small and more or less disappears a mile south of St. Raphaël, below which point the stream exhibits characteristics of rejuvenation.

Different from the areas discussed above, yet included within the region because of their aridity, are great ranges of limestone which form the western and northeastern margins of the plain. Smaller, isolated limestone hills also occur within the central part of the region.

In all these hills the overburden is extremely shallow or even non-existent (Plate 18). Many areas are indeed almost completely barren. Others support a low cover of shrubs and trees, which are xerophytic at lower elevations and semi-deciduous at higher altitudes. Nevertheless, there are also extensive areas in which some cultivation is attempted. Few limestone slopes will not support some manioc or guinea grass or a few plants of beans and corn, and scattered clearings may be seen over at least half of the hillsides. South of La Victoire, several narrow basins carved in beds of shale or soft limestone have deeper soils and are devoted largely to sugar cane and corn.

In examining population distribution in the region, it is at once evident that most of the people live in the plateau or in basins within the limestone. Only in the extreme north, where the hills are so broad that some sections are rather inaccessible from the plain, have many dwellings been built on the uplands.

Even on the plateau, however, the pattern of settlement is not uniform, but exhibits local variations in response to the productivity of land and the availability of water. Of the two factors, the former is the more important; the number of dwellings in each area and its carrying capacity are almost perfectly correlated. Particularly dense concentrations of houses are seen in and around the main irrigated area, west of the Bouyaha, and in places where smaller mountain streams descend to the plain. Although these streams do not flow throughout the year, they permit seasonal irrigation, and contribute appreciably to ground water supplies. In contrast, relatively few huts are located near the lower Bouyaha which, though dependable, is too deeply incised into the plateau to be useful for irrigation. Gravel terraces and limestone plains with shallow soils are almost uninhabited.

SUMMARY

In the analysis of rural land utilization and settlement, most of the areal differences in the intensity and types of agriculture, in the vegetation of uncropped areas, and in the locations of dwellings may be related directly to variations in elements of the physical environment, such as the texture, fertility, and drainage of soils, the depth of the overburden, the gradients, and the amount and seasonal distribution of precipitation.

Human factors, such as the system of land tenure, the agricultural techniques used, and the initiative taken in land improvement also play an important part in the formation of the land use pattern. These influences, however, are relatively constant throughout the Département, and even where they vary man's activities are seen to be closely related to the physical qualities of the land.

7. Towns, Villages, and Markets

ALTHOUGH only a very small proportion of the total area of the Département du Nord is built up, the towns, villages, and markets merit special attention (Figure 15). Not only do they contain nearly one-seventh of the population of the Département, but in their distribution and functions, they provide the major clues to an understanding of the relationships between the geographic regions which were discussed in the preceding chapter.

The implied distinction between towns and villages is rather arbitrary, for even the larger places of concentrated settlement include among their residents a large number of farmers. To reach their fields, these farmers daily travel, usually on foot, distances up to about four miles each way. In most cases, however, the journey is much shorter. As is indicated by the population map of the Département, most of the towns are surrounded by belts in which rural population densities are relatively low, but these belts are generally not over half a mile in width. Evidently, few farmers are willing to suffer a greater separation from their land in order to benefit by the few urban amenities which exist. Among these amenities, the most important are schools, churches, and a few shops. Otherwise, the towns have little to offer. Except as noted hereunder, urban houses are similar to rural houses, while the organized supply of water, removal of wastes, and protection against fire are virtually unknown everywhere.

Clearly, the Haitian peasantry is not markedly gregarious. Villages are not required as dwelling places for farmers, but have arisen to exercise other functions.

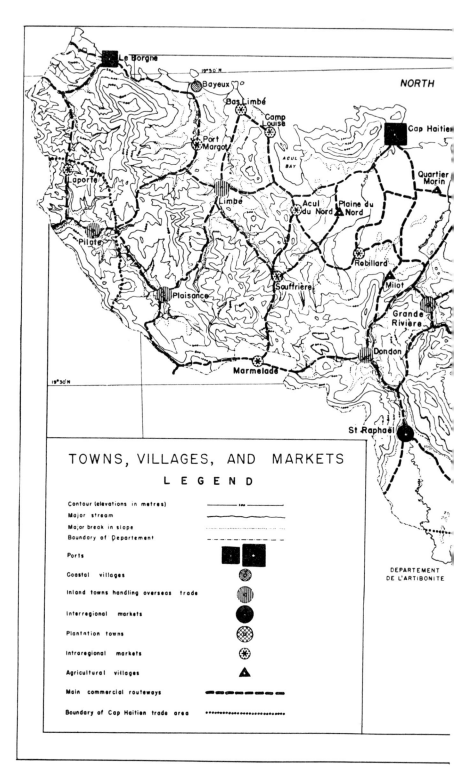

Figure 15. Towns, Villages, and Markets

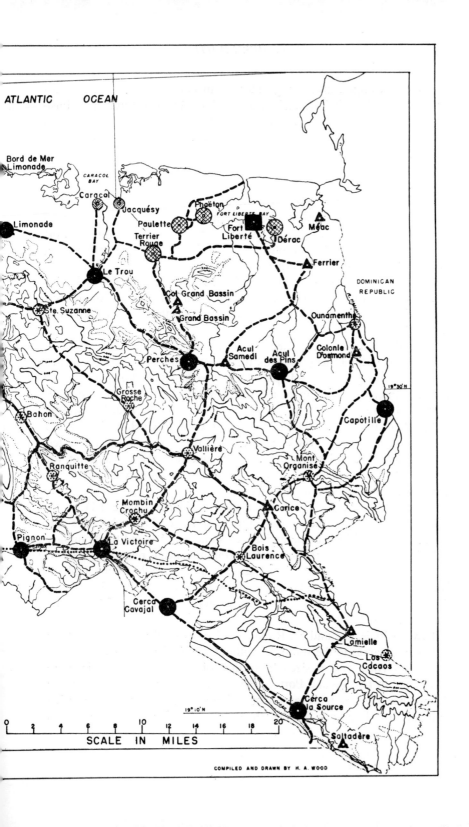

ATLANTIC   OCEAN

Bord de Mer
Limonade

CARACOL
BAY

Caracol

Jacquésy

Phaëton

FORT LIBERTÉ BAY

Fort
Liberté

Dérac

Méac

Limonade

Paulette

Terrier
Rouge

Le Trou

Ste. Suzanne

Ferrier

Col Grand Bassin

Grand Bassin

Ounamenthe

DOMINICAN
REPUBLIC

Perches

Acul
Samedi

Acul
des Pins

Colonie
D'osmond

Grosse
Roche

19°30'N

Bahon

Vallière

Capotille

Ranquitte

Mont
Organisé

Mombin
Crochu

Carice

Pignon

La Victoire

Bois
Laurence

Cerca
Cavajal

Lamielle

Los
Cacaos

19°10'N

Cerca
la Source

Saltadère

0   2   4   6   8   10   12   14   16   18   20

SCALE   IN   MILES

COMPILED AND DRAWN BY H. A. WOOD

Ports

By far the strongest urbanizing influence in Haiti is overseas trade, for
commerce of this kind is handled by a relatively small number of business houses and is funnelled through a few points along the coast. From
the days of earliest European setlement, the bulk of this interchange
has been centred on Cap Haitien (population in 1950, 24,229), and
this town is now more than six times as large as any other in the
Département.

The main assets of Cap Haitien are its harbour, its centrality, and its
relatively easy contact with the best agricultural sections of the Département. The harbour, though not as landlocked or as spacious as Fort
Liberté Bay, affords good protection for shipping and is, furthermore,
adjacent to the humid western part of the Plaine du Nord, which was
the main cultivated area in colonial days. From Cap Haitien it is also
posible to travel not only over the coastal plain but also, by low passes,
into fertile valleys and basins to the west and into the Central Plateau to
the south.

Some difficulty was experienced in linking the town site with the
mainland. Reaching away towards the eastern and southern sections of
the Département is the sand spit which separates Cap Haitien harbour
from the mangrove swamp to the south, yet the spit was cut off from
the townsite by the Haut du Cap River. The route westward along the
north side of the river was blocked by a rocky spur which projected into
the swamp. But the river was bridged, the tip of the spur was blasted
away, and Cap Haitien became without question the focal point for
northeast Haiti. Commercially and culturally the town now dominates an
area nearly as extensive as the Département which it administers. The
two areas are, nevertheless, not exactly coincident (Figure 15).

To the northwest, the contact provided by trading schooners has
extended Cap Haitien's commercial area somewhat beyond the boundary
of the Département, but this zone of coastal influence is relatively shallow.
Inland, the basin of the Trois Rivières is as accessible to the Gulf of
Gonave as it is to the Atlantic. Therefore, while Cap Haitien is the port
of the eastern section of the Basin, its western area is served largely by
Gonaïves.

Between Plaisance and St. Raphaël, all parts of the Département, as
well as small areas to the south, lie within Cap Haitien's zone of domination, but farther east a sizeable section of the Département is more
closely tied to Hinche and Port-au-Prince. The divide between the zones
of influence runs roughly east from Pignon and La Victoire, passing
south of Bois Laurence, but north of Lamielle. Significantly, no road

follows the shale valley linking Cerca la Source with La Victoire and the area to the north. The only highway into the Cerca la Source Basin enters from the south.

While, therefore, one might profitably relocate some portions of the boundary of the area administratively controlled from Cap Haitien,[1] on the whole the correlation between the areas of political, economic, and cultural domination is as close as is to be found in most areas of similar size and complexity. Competition from other centres is no threat to Cap Haitien, and its position as departmental centre is secure.

The town does face problems, yet these stem not from its regional situation, but from the constriction of its site. The town is crammed onto a narrow piedmont fan and marine terrace, beyond which it cannot expand, to the east because of the bay, to the south because of the swamp, and to the north and west because of precipitous slopes. The streets, which follow a fairly regular grid pattern, are only twenty to thirty feet wide; houses are built right up the street lines and balconies often overhang the roadway. There are some interior courtyards, but these are usually small, dank, and malodorous.

The congestion extends also into individual buildings, as most rooms are subdivided by newspaper screens into cubicles barely large enough to take a bed. One room or less per family is all that is available for 53 per cent of the households of the town. Sewer and water systems of a sort exist, but only 13 per cent of the buildings have private connections with the water mains and less than 5 per cent have interior toilets.[2] Most buildings are of masonry, though many are of frame construction. Roofs are of tile and sheet metal, thatch being prohibited by law because of the danger of fire.

This congestion, however, does not prevent Cap Haitien from carrying out its major functions. Facilities are adequate for the storage and handling, collection and distribution of goods entering overseas trade, while, to maintain the food supply, there is a large daily market. The town has high schools, a hospital, and a variety of light industries in addition to many government offices. Recently the streets have been paved, a new pier has been built to handle small ocean-going ships, and a waterfront boulevard has been constructed on reclaimed land.

In addition to Cap Haitien, the Département contains two smaller ports. The older of these is Fort Liberté (population 800) which, during

---

[1]This relocation has already been accomplished by the army and the national health service, both of which administer the southeastern part of the Département from Hinche, rather than from Cap Haitien.

[2]Figures from the general census of 1950.

the colonial period, was the commercial centre for an area of irrigated agriculture in the Massacre plain. Substantial buildings, broad streets, wide squares, and a regular plan proclaimed its essentially urban character. Yet expulsion of the French brought a decay of the irrigation works and a collapse of overseas trade which destroyed the town's economy. Now the most imposing structures are in ruins. Shops are few, and the small market provides food not for an extensive region, but only for the townspeople. However, Fort Liberté is still the administrative centre of an arrondissement, and civil servants help bolster the population. It also still retains the legal status of a port; all shipments of sisal from Dérac and Phaëton are listed officially as exports from Fort Liberté. Even though the goods never pass through Fort Liberté, they are cleared by the customs house there.

Fort Liberté is also the official port of entry for petroleum products which are actually unloaded at Brisson Point, at the entrance to Fort Liberté Bay. The main reason for the selection of this site for the dock and storage tanks is that on the entire coast of the Département this is the only sheltered haven in which a large tanker can come close to shore; only 175 yards separate the littoral from the ten-fathom line. However, the barren nature of the site, and its remoteness from populated areas, make it unsuitable for a general port. The only people who live here permanently are a superintendent and his family. Brisson Point is therefore not classed as a town in its own right, though it fulfils an urban function. From here gasoline, diesel oil, and fuel oil are distributed to all parts of the Département except Pilate, Pignon, and Cerca la Source, these remote towns being supplied from Port-au-Prince. The two last-named products are also sent from Brisson Point to nearby sections of the Dominican Republic.

Farther west, direct overseas shipments are effected from the sisal factory at Madras, on Caracol Bay, yet here, too, the permanent population consists only of a few watchmen. Customs clearance is provided from Cap Haitien, and Madras cannot be considered to be an urban centre despite its function.

The newer of the Département's two small ports is Le Borgne (population 1,325). Located in the west, about as far from Cap Haitien as is Fort Liberté to the east, Le Borgne is at the seaward end of the Borgne valley, the only easy outlet for the products of the rich agricultural area south of the coastal hills. The town is built on the neck of a tombolo, and, though little shelter is available for large ships, small schooners find an adequate harbour in the mouth of the Rivière du Borgne. Le Borgne's main function is the grading, packing, and shipping of coffee and cacao from the Borgne Coffee District. These products are sent to Cap Haitien, in part by truck, but mainly by boat, and are there picked up by the ocean-going vessels which do not find it economic to stop at Le Borgne. The only period during which direct overseas shipments were regularly made from Le Borgne was during the Second World War. At that time, bananas were grown for export in the Borgne Coffee District, and ships called at the port to load this perishable fruit.

With its grid pattern of streets and its masonry buildings and warehouses, Le Borgne has a distinctly urban appearance. It has many small shops and a small daily market to meet the needs of the urban residents as well as a larger market twice weekly for people of surrounding rural areas.

Coastal Villages

The activities of these residential seaside communities were discussed in the preceding chapter. Located at points accessible both to land and sea, they include such places as Bayeux (population 150), Bord de Mer Limonade (population 700), Caracol (population 520) and Jacquésy (population 540). Because of their peripheral location, they have little or no commercial life, and many of their residents work on nearby commercial plantations.

Plantation Towns

The four communities of this type are located around Fort Liberté Bay. Two, Phaëton (population 1,730) and Dérac (population 2,490), have a mixed industrial-agricultural population. The two others, Paulette (population 2,470) and Terrier Rouge (population 2,400), are inhabited almost exclusively by field workers. Because most of the residents of these communities must purchase all their food, markets are held daily at Dérac and Paulette, the latter market serving also Phaëton and Terrier Rouge. Because commerce occupies a subsidiary position in the urban economy, the market-places are located on the fringes rather than in the centres of the towns.

Each of these four towns, except Terrier Rouge, which is not located on plantation property, includes a section of company-built houses which are tiny but neat, of masonry construction and laid out in rows. The three also contain quarters with native-built huts of small sticks and palm leaves woven together, many without benefit even of a coat of mud. These dwellings are unquestionably the poorest to be found in the Département. In contrast, Phaëton and Dérac also possess modern detached houses, set in spacious park-like surroundings, for foreign supervisory personnel.

Inland Towns Handling Overseas Trade

Although the final preparation of goods for export is carried out in the ports, there are a few inland centres at which a preliminary collection and grading is carried out. The exercise of these functions gives a distinctive appearance to a town. It has many masonry storehouses, small retail stores carrying foodstuffs, cloth, and hardware, and quite substantial homes of merchants. These buildings are usually loosely grouped around the main market square and surrounded by dwellings of artisans and labourers, which are constructed largely of wattle with metal roofing.

In addition, these towns also serve as points for the exchange of local agricultural and manufactured products. They are, therefore, bustling with activity on market-days, though they are fairly busy on other days as well. The Département contains five towns of this type, all in the humid western area, since this area produces the bulk of the most important peasant export crop: coffee.

In two cases, the trade areas of these collecting centres coincide fairly well with geographic regions. Dondon (population 1,689) receives the coffee of its basin and the surrounding hills. Limbé (population 3,744) serves the Limbé Valley as well as the two valleys which meet just above the town. The Plaisance Garden, however, has two commercial centres because the trade of the area is divided between Cap Haitien and Gonaïves. Coffee moving to the former is collected at Plaisance (population 1,692), that destined to the latter is assembled at Pilate (population 1,280).

The most easterly town of this group, Grande Rivière (population 2,696), differs somewhat from the other four as, in addition to collecting coffee from its immediate hinterland, it is also a marketing point for some cotton fibre and cottonseed from parts of the Central Plateau to the south of the Département du Nord. These commodities were originally brought into Grande Rivière from Pignon by pack animals which were able to negotiate the direct route offered by the middle section of the Grande Rivière valley and the gorge of one of its southern tributaries. This route, however, does not lend itself to road construction, and when, in the 1930's, a motor road was built linking the Plateau with the Plaine du Nord, it followed a more devious course, passing through St. Raphaël and Dondon but bypassing Grande Rivière. The diversion of much trade to this new route has had a depressing effect on Grande Rivière. It seems somewhat less active than the other centres of this group, even though its many substantial buildings make it the most urban in appearance.

All five towns are located on natural transportation corridors. They are also not quite centrally situated in their areas of supply, being slightly displaced in the direction of the port city. It is also worthy of note that no towns of this type exist within a radius of twelve miles of Cap Haitien. Coffee produced in the Acul Piedmont and adjacent areas may be efficiently marketed directly in the port.

Interregional Markets

These places are the great centres for the exchange of domestic food-stuffs and manufactured articles. They are located, not to the west with the inland towns handling overseas trade, but to the east, where food production is most highly seasonal and where, during most of the year, many people must buy food in order to live. Furthermore, the east, in addition to mountains and basins, also contains extensive plain and plateau sections, each with a distinctive crop pattern and each requiring, at times, the products of the others.

In the west, on the other hand, all areas are much more self-sufficient. Although a considerable volume of local trade exists, it is less essential than in the east, and the main commercial centres, as indicated above, are oriented largely towards overseas trade.

Consequently, all communities which serve principally and most conspicuously as interregional markets are located in areas less humid than Climatic Type III. They all lie, furthermore, near the boundary between the areas which generally have food surpluses and the areas generally deficient in food, and also near the divide between areas of high and low relief. They are thus disposed in two distinct rows. Each row has five markets and the spacing between the markets is remarkably uniform. To the north of the Massif, along the border of the Plaine du Nord, are Limonade (population 1,208), Le Trou (population 2,879), Perches (population 935), Acul des Pins (population 150), and Capotille (population 150). To the south, on the margin or on outliers of the Central Plateau, are St. Raphaël (population 1,459), Pignon (population 1,546), La Victoire (population 670), Cerca Cavajal (population *c.* 300) and Cerca la Source (population 530). Of these, the fourth mentioned lies in a salient of the Département de l'Artibonite, but is none the less an integral member of the group.

All these centres are distinguished by the large size of their market-places. Each of these covers several acres of ground and is equipped with rows of small booths, which are rented by the vendors. At each centre, markets are held on two or three days each week, different days being commonly used at adjacent towns. For this reason, and because of the lack of agricultural homogeneity in this area, there is a considerable overlapping of trade territories. However, the maximum distance which people normally travel each way is about twenty miles. Those who come the maximum distance leave home in the forenoon of the day preceding the market, arrive in the evening, and sleep in the market-place beside their wares. Trading begins at daybreak and is usually completed by midmorning giving the people time to return home before nightfall.

Although these markets are of immense importance to the rural populace, they are not strong urbanizing influences. Since most people come not just to buy or sell, but to exchange one product for another, little cash is left over for the purchase of imported goods. For this reason, and because of the short duration of the market, its existence does not contribute greatly to local employment. Some women prepare and sell meals on market days, tradesmen such as tailors and shoe-makers may pick up a little business, but permanent shops are tiny and few. Most of the people with homes in these towns contribute little to the functioning of the market.

It is possible, therefore, for settlements of this type to vary considerably in the size of their permanent populations. Some, such as Limonade, Le Trou, St. Raphaël, and Pignon, located in agriculturally productive areas, are inhabited by over a thousand people. Others, such as Acul des Pins and Capotille, in drier sections with less fertile soils, have scarcely any permanent residents at all.

But in the poorer areas as well as in the richer, these markets are needed, and within the two rows at the base of the mountains, their locations are determined less by the quality of the site than by considerations of accessibility. The markets must be spaced out so as to serve the entire eastern part of the Département. Hence the distance between adjacent centres in each row is in most cases about eight miles. Only Pignon and La Victoire are significantly closer, and the latter in consequence has a smaller market than other towns of this group. Only Cerca la Source and Cerca Cavajal are much farther apart (about twelve miles) due to the low population and low productivity of the intervening country.

All these markets are also located at or near places where routeways running along the margins of the Massif lie opposite passes across the mountains. This principle of location, however, as well as those mentioned above, may be slightly modified to permit the establishment of a market near a water supply. Only one of these centres, Acul des Pins, is not near a permanent stream.

It is interesting to observe that no line of major markets runs north and south between the humid area to the west and the drier area to the east. Although St. Raphaël, Dondon, and Limonade do carry on some trade between east and west, it is clear that this exchange is much smaller in volume than the internal commerce within each of the two divisions. There must therefore be a considerable measure of self-sufficiency in the subhumid as well as in the humid parts of the Département. The large quantity of trade in the east reflects local deficiencies, often of specific products, rather than an over-all food shortage.

Intraregional Markets
The towns handling overseas trade and the interregional markets, with their broad general exchange of goods, do not adequately serve all the commercial needs of the people of the Département. In many districts the local inhabitants engage in some additional trade. If a region has a surplus of food, outsiders will come to obtain it; if there is known to be a deficiency, people will come in to sell. There has, therefore, developed a complementary group of commercial centres to serve areas relatively remote from the markets discussed above.

The spacing of these places is somewhat less rigid than that of the larger market centres, but is subject, in part, to the same general principles. Eight miles is maintained fairly constantly as the maximum distance between markets, though the distance is often less in areas of above-average productivity, or where physiographic barriers intervene. Thus Port Margot is only four miles from Limbé, and Mombin Crochu is but three miles from La Victoire, but in both cases the two nearby centres lies in adjacent valleys separated by steep ridges. Also in the humid western section of the Département, the average distance between market towns drops from eight miles to six.

All of these markets require a location on or near major trade routes and in a reasonably productive agricultural area. Generally speaking, one or other of these characteristics predominates. Robillard, Bas Limbé, Acul du Nord (population 1,231), Port Margot (population 1,160), and Ounamenthe (population 2,200) are in some of the best agricultural areas of the Département. The first two, in level homogeneous terrain, are merely market-places surrounded by dense rural populations, but without any continuously built-up areas. The last three, on well-drained eminences near poorly drained depressions, are towns of considerable size.

Those towns which owe their trade primarily to their accessibility include Bahon (population 672), Mont Organisé (population 541), Ranquitte (population 580), Bois Laurence (population 145), Ste.

Suzanne (population 381), Camp Louise (population 150), Souffrière (population 150), Vallière (population 310), Mombin Crochu (population 290), Grosse Roche (population 150), Los Cacaos (population 30), and Laporte (population 150). Of these, the first three have relatively large populations because they lie on the two main routes through the mountains and have acquired some long-distance commerce in addition to their regional trade.

It might be noted that Terrier Rouge was once one of these local market towns, but it has lost its trade to the new market at Paulette and is now, as indicated above, essentially a village of sisal workers.

Agricultural Villages

Communities of this category, despite their interior locations, have negligible commercial functions. They may have small markets, but these serve only the people of the community and not those of the surrounding area; several have no markets at all.

Instead of the more normal, dispersed rural settlement, these villages have developed in a few places in response to specific local conditions. Thus, poor drainage has compeled farmers in several areas to live together wherever higher ground is to be found; the villages formed in this way include Plaine du Nord (population 560), Carice (population 220), Ferrier (population 1,125), and Méac (population 180). In an area of low productivity a pocket of good soil may be a localizing influence as at Lamielle (population 150), Saltadère (population 140), Grand Bassin (population 470), and Acul Samedi (population 150).

Human affairs also play a part in the location of these villages. Milot (population 1,179) exists today mainly because the former king Christophe built his palace here, at the base of the hills, in a straight line between his economic capital, Cap Haitien, and his military redoubt, the Citadelle. Quartier Morin (population 604) is a compact settlement because so much land has been acquired for the commercial production of sugar, sisal, and bananas that people have been forced to congregate together, especially at crossroads such as this, accessible to most of the plantations. The refugee colonies of d'Osmond (population 450) and Grand Bassin (population 540) were set up by state planners.

These examples do not by any means exhaust the list of agricultural communities, but all major types are covered, and the places which are not mentioned have no urban characteristics other than high population density.

Military and Administrative Centres

Almost all the larger communities mentioned above possess some government offices and exercise an administrative function in some degree. This function, however, is usually clearly subordinate to commercial or residential functions. It has been a result, rather than a cause, of urban development.

There are, nevertheless, three towns which have attained their present size and importance, largely because they were selected as centres of administration. Two of these towns, Ounamenthe and Cerca la Source, are military centres. They are the only sizeable communities in the Département close to the international border, yet easily accessible. They are both garrisoned by strong army detachments.

The third town of this group is Vallière, which is a centre of civic administration. Because it is the only village in the east-central part of the Massif, Vallière has been designated the capital of an arrondissement, and without its complement of civil servants, it would not have attained even its present modest population of 450.

SUMMARY

All the urban centres of the Département du Nord exist essentially to serve the needs of the agricultural population or to handle agricultural products. Therefore, all these centres are influenced, even though indirectly, by the climatic and edaphic factors which were observed to have an effect upon the type of crop grown and the yields obtained.

The urban pattern within the Département indicates that commerce is well established everywhere. This trade permits the peasants to practise some degree of agricultural specialization, as has been noted in the previous chapter. No one is compelled by a system of complete self-sufficiency to produce all the commodities which he expects to consume. But since the requirements of the native farmers are extremely simple, only a rudimentary hierarchy of commercial towns has developed. In this hierarchy no more than three orders may be distinguished. The third or lowest order comprises the intraregional markets, which are spaced no more than eight miles apart. One first-order town exists, namely Cap Haitien, the main commercial and administrative centre of the Département. The second order includes agglomerations of two types. Those of the humid west are substantial towns dealing in coffee and other items entering international trade. Those of the drier east are intermittently active markets in which food and native manufactures are the main commodities bought and sold. Because the two groups of second-order centres have different requirements for services and permanent installations, those of the east are considerably smaller than those of the west.

The Département also contains settlements with little or no commercial activities. Inhabited by farmers, fishermen, or industrial workers, these communities are located primarily with reference to the quality of the terrain and the conditions of work. They are not essential to the functioning of the Département as a whole.

8. Conclusions

AN EXAMINATION of the physical and human geography of the Département du Nord, Republic of Haiti, indicates that this densely populated section of the humid tropics possesses a great diversity of geologic, climatic, vegetational, and edaphic elements, but is essentially homogeneous in its racial, social, and cultural characteristics. The economy is also fairly uniform. Peasant agriculture, carried out with primitive techniques, dominates everywhere except in some commercial plantations of the coastal lowlands and in an irrigated section of the interior plateau. In some places farming is supplemented by forestry and fishing, but these activities are of very minor importance.

Even the urban pattern, except for a few communities of sisal workers, is tributary to peasant agriculture. Though the sites of town are determined largely by accessibility, drainage, and water supply, their sizes, functions, and spacing are basically in response to the type, volume, and seasonality of agricultural production.

Here, then, is an area with activities, cultural levels, and living standards comparable with those found in many primitive parts of the world, and one in which human development may be related with particular clarity to the physical landscape. Here it is possible to appreciate the relations between the land and its people both qualitatively and quantitatively. Rock, soil, months of wet weather, and months of drought can be expressed in terms of the crops which will grow, the proportion of the land which can be cultivated, the number of people who are able to gain their livelihood from each square mile, and the occurrence of seasonal food shortages. Among the many relationships of this kind which are evident in the Département, the most important are the following:

In the northwest, where no months are dry, tree crops such as coffee and cacao do particularly well, while the planting and harvesting of corn, sugar cane, plantains, taro, yams, manioc, sweet potatoes, and other vegetables proceed without seasonal interruptions on soils of all types. Of all the common food crops, only rice is seasonal in its growth; even these areas experience seasons of minimum rainfall during which rice will thrive only in lagoons or in other areas with a high water table.

Where one month is dry, the only crop which disappears is cacao and, for the others, seasonality of production is imposed only in sandy soils. Where two months are dry, the same crops are grown, but year-round production occurs only on clay soils. In places with three dry months, all cultivation of annual plants is on a seasonal basis, while coffee and plantains may be grown only on favoured sites. Four successive dry months are fatal to both coffee and plantains; under these conditions the only crops which can survive throughout the year are manioc, sugar cane, sisal, and castor beans.

The control exercised upon agriculture by climate is intensified by the fact that the amount and distribution of rainfall influence not only plant growth but also the land itself. The longer the period of drought, the slower the rate of rock disintegration and the longer the interval of rest required for the land after each period of cultivation. Even during the rainy season, therefore, the intensity of land use differs from place to place.

In the humid northwest, the best land is planted every year while poorer fields are usually cultivated about two years out of three. In contrast, regularly farmed sections of the drier parts of the Département are actually under crops only about one year in three. Some areas are so unfavourable for agriculture that a rest period of five to ten years may be required after each year of cultivation; under these circumstances, land holdings are not only relatively large but rather ill-defined.

The limitations imposed upon agriculture give rise, in turn, to periodic shortages of food, and, outside of a few irrigated areas, the existence and severity of such shortages depend both on the number of wet months and the number of dry months. Generally speaking, unless the wet season is at least six months in duration, food deficiencies are more common than food surpluses, but, with two exceptions, even the driest parts of the Département experience some periods of abundance. The exceptions are the area of shale outcroppings in the extreme southeast and the zone of sisal plantations in the northeast, where commercial production of this fibre crop has attracted a larger number of people than the land could otherwise support.

With a wet season six or seven months long, food surpluses tend to be more common than food deficiencies, though deficiencies are rare or unknown only in areas where no months are dry. Both of these generalizations, however, require qualification due to the influence of soils. Places with particularly droughty or infertile soils may experience severe and prolonged food shortages even though seven months of the year are wet and occasional deficiencies even in areas where no months are dry. On the other hand, there are a few places with particularly fine soils where, even though one month each year is dry, food shortages seldom occur.

The magnitude of the influence of climate upon agriculture does not mean, however, that soils, with their associated consolidated and unconsolidated parent materials, are relatively unimportant. Edaphic factors do, in fact, control land use in ways which are everywhere significant and in some places paramount. For this reason, most of the generalizations made concerning the relations between climate and food production have had to be qualified to take cognizance of variations in soil properties, and the effects of these variations must now be systematically summarized.

In areas with transported parent materials, the most important variables are moisture supply and retention and the chemical characteristics of the soil. Excessive or imperfect internal soil drainage, as has been suggested, has the effect of increasing or mitigating the severity of the dry season. Agriculturally, an area with excessively drained soil may be no better than one with normal drainage and a dry season one or even two months longer. Similarly, imperfect drainage, if accompanied by good moisture storage, reduces the effective length of the dry season by about one month. Imperfect drainage also exerts a more selective influence in that it inhibits the production of manioc, coffee, and cacao, but may be advantageous, especially in drier areas, for crops such as rice.

Drainage, in turn, is related largely to soil texture, though, as is normally the case, the coarser the texture the more variable the moisture relationships. Sand and gravel in flood plains may be adequately supplied with water whereas similar deposits on nearby terraces may be extremely droughty.

The chemical content of the soil may also affect its moisture retention, specifically in places where the presence of salts in excessive amounts produces an impermeable hardpan. The more general significance of soil chemicals, however, is in the indication they provide that the parent materials are breaking down into forms suitable for absorption by plants. In general, the finer the particles in the soil, the more complete the breakdown, the higher the fertility and the larger the crop yields. The clays, silts, and loams of the alluvial and marine deposits of the Département tend, therefore, to be more fertile than the areas of sand or gravel, and, unless poorly drained, to be more productive.

An additional factor, however, is the origin of the materials. Those derived from the erosion of volcanic formations are richer in plant nutrients than those derived from other types of rock. This phenomenon is strikingly illustrated by the high fertility of piedmont fans formed below basalt slopes even though the material of the fans is quite coarse.

In areas of residual soils developed on bedrock, the most important variable is the depth of the overburden. Wherever this depth was found to be in excess of four feet, the land was susceptible to gully erosion, mature soils were highly leached and too sterile for most crops, and even youthful soils were only moderately productive. With overburden less than four feet in depth, leaching does not appear to be a serious problem, and even on clean cultivated hillsides with slopes of over 60 per cent, gullies were not observed except in areas of quartz diorite, where there is a high clay content in the soil. Very shallow overburden, however, is a disadvantage; where it is less than six inches thick, coffee and plantains do not thrive, and a long rest period is required for the land, during which time guinea grass is often used as a cover crop. Where there is less than two inches of unconsolidated material, agriculture becomes impossible.

The optimum range in the depth of overburden is, therefore, from six inches to four feet, but since the conditions under which these depths are found, and the agricultural productivity of the soil, are directly related to bedrock types, the more important of these will be briefly examined.

The granite of the Département weathers to produce a layer of coarse quartz sand which is quite infertile. Furthermore, where the relief is low and the dry season pronounced, a laterite hardpan commonly develops at depths of six to eighteen inches within the soil. These soils are essentially non-agricultural. Granitic areas without laterite are mainly in forest; those with laterite have a cover of coarse grass.

The soils developed on quartz diorite also contain many quartz crystals, but they are held in a massive matrix of clay. Depth to bedrock is one to three feet, moisture retention is good, but fertility is low. Most areas of quartz diorite are cultivated regularly; the most common crops are the tolerant manioc, rice, and beans.

Upon andesite the eroding regolith is renewed so rapidly by the weathering of the bedrock that it may be considered to be almost indestructible. Even on cultivated slopes of over 70 per cent, there exists a continuous layer of overburden at least one foot deep, and in most areas the depth to bedrock is three to four feet. The soils, freshly formed from rock rich in plant nutrients, are fertile. They produce all the common crops of the Département, and where they occur in dry areas they support islands of cultivation surrounded by stretches of woods or pasture.

Basalt weathers even more rapidly than andesite, but the weathering is accompanied by sheet erosion so severe that the overburden is found to be quite shallow, generally from six to twelve inches in depth, and thus rather droughty. Nevertheless, virtually all the land is used for agriculture. The main crops are guinea grass, manioc, and sweet potatoes.

The limestone weathers unevenly to form pockets of fertile soil up to twenty inches in depth interspersed with pinnacles and ridges of rock. Despite their forbidding appearance, these areas can be productive, and all crops are grown. Their main disadvantage is that travel through them is very difficult.

On the shale, the soils are more varied than in the other types of bedrock due to the greater influence of climate upon the rate of weathering. Indeed, where the wet season is under six months in length, this rate is too slow to support agriculture on hill slopes except on the basis of a long-term land rotation. Where the wet season is less than four months in duration, the overburden is everywhere too shallow for any farming. However, in more humid shale areas, one finds up to two or three feet of residual silt loam even on steep cultivated slopes. A variety of crops can be grown, but the most characteristic is corn, for which these soils are particularly well suited chemically.

The final point to consider is the effect of the foregoing upon population distribution. Here narrow generalizations may be misleading as the techniques used in house construction limit the choice of sites to fairly level areas, while the danger of floods and the availability of water are futher locative factors for dwellings. Some of the best farmland in the Département has few houses built on it, while sizeable villages may occupy relatively poor land. Nevertheless, it is evident that the human carrying capacity of the land is mainly a function of the length of the dry season. In areas with fewer than two dry months per year the best land supports over 800 persons per square mile while densities of over 400 per square mile are found everywhere except on rugged limestone hills and in places with lateritic soils. On the other hand, where the dry season exceeds two months in duration, population densities are less than 200 per square mile except in areas of low relief with heavy-textured soils or a high water table. Where soils are particularly shallow or sterile, there are less than 100 persons per square mile.

It is clear, therefore, that throughout the Département du Nord, the peasant farmers have worked out an extremely fine adjustment between their use of the land and its physical characteristics. The only areas which are not fully utilized are some rather infertile or inaccessible mountain peaks, and a few pockets of arable land within plains of laterite. The peaks are neglected because their cultivation would entail a greater expenditure of time and energy in travelling than the meagre returns would justify. In the case of the small undeveloped patches on the laterite plains, their full potential may not yet have been discovered by the peasantry.

The relation between peasant agriculture and land potential is not only close but also stable. Except in a few shale areas recently cleared of forest, fields are adequately rested between periods of cultivation, and the demands made on the land do not exceed its capacity to satisfy them. However, it is not possible for greater demands to be met without agricultural advances. These might include the introduction of new quick-growing crop varieties and the use of fertilizers. Some erosion control on slopes might also be introduced to permit a reduction in the length of the rest period which is now needed for building up the depth of the overburden as well as for restoring its fertility.

In some respects, the conclusions reached with respect to peasant agriculture may also be applied to commercial plantations, though the latter exhibit a dependence upon slope and accessibility which the former do not. It is important to note, however, that plantations have brought local economic advantages only where sisal has been introduced in areas which are too dry to produce significant quantities of food. In more humid parts of the Département plantations have brought no over-all benefits, at least from the point of view of the worker on the land. Plantation hands are no more prosperous than peasant farmers, and a square mile of plantations support fewer people than a square mile of comparable productivity used for peasant farms. Of the two systems of land tenure, peasant agriculture is the stronger competitor for the land; plantations are not only relatively small and scattered but tend to be short-lived.

Only in two areas does it appear that a shift away from peasant agriculture might be of benefit to the people. One is in the northeast where some extension of sisal production is possible. The other is in the pine forests of the southeast where some land might well be set aside exclusively for the production of timber. Nevertheless, even if these changes were made, less than ten per cent of the Département would be affected. In the future as in the present, the peasant farmer will remain the principal figure in the population and in the economy of the Département du Nord, and the principles which govern his use of the land will always be the most important geographical relationships in this part of the Republic of Haiti.

These land use principles may also be applied in many other areas of the humid tropics, for in Haiti the peasants have been given a freer hand than in almost any other part of the modern world. Without external control, guidance, or assistance, they have worked within the universal frame of reference provided by the endurance of the human frame, the solid material of the earth's crust, and the moisture which falls from the skies. What they have achieved should not be beyond the grasp of primitive people in comparable environments anywhere on earth.

Appendices

The granite of the Département du Nord is coarsely crystalline and composed mainly of quartz, hornblende, and orthoclase. The quartz diorite has smaller crystals; andesine is its major constituent, averaging 46 per cent of the total volume, while quartz and hornblende each contribute about 23 per cent.[1]

The basalts are typically fine-grained, their major mineral consituents being augite and labradorite.[2]

The andesites are fine-grained to dense or glassy and are more variable in composition than the basalts. Their most common minerals are labradorite, andesine,[3] albite, anorthite and oligoclase.[4]

A typical exposure of shale is described as follows: "The beds are 2 to 5 centimetres in thickness and very regular. They consist of indurated dark brown fine-grained sandstone or slaty shale."[5] Silica is the major chemical constituent, comprising over 50 per cent of the total.

Most of the limestone in the Département is of a massive type described as: "hard . . . grey on weathered and white on fresh surfaces. It occurs in reasonably regular beds, ranging in thickness from 10 to 30 centimetres, but on weathered slopes or bluffs it usually appears massive. The beds contain little or no shale or other detrital material and generally very little chert."[6]

There are also examples of different types of limestone described as: "white to yellow (with a) porous, chalky or sandy appearance although unweathered specimens are rather hard. The beds are generally regular and even and most of them range from 5 to 15 centimetres in thickness. Shaly partings are common, and some beds contain sandy detrital material and even coarse conglomerate."[7]

[1]Woodring *et al.*, *Geology*, p. 292.
[2]Butterlin, *Géologie*, p. 41.
[3]*Ibid.*, p. 42.
[4]*Ibid.*
[5]Woodring *et al.*, *Geology*, p. 87.
[6]*Ibid.*, p. 108.
[7]*Ibid.*

B. CLIMATIC STATISTICS*

List of Stations

(For locations see Figure 11)

1. Le Borgne	6. Cap Haitien	10. Botany	14. Grande Rivière
2. Bayeux	7. Bonnay	11. Bonnement	15. Bahon
3. Pilate	8. Limonade	12. Ounamenthe	16. Dondon
4. Plaisance	9. Le Trou	13. Vallière	17. St. Raphaël
5. Limbé			18. Cerca la Source

Station Number	Years Recorded	J	F	M	A	M	J	J	A	S	O	N	D	Year
					Mean Rainfall in Inches								
1	22	7.12	5.39	5.14	6.93	6.17	3.94	2.76	2.65	4.40	8.30	14.51	7.63	74.93
2	18	4.58	4.67	4.42	7.28	8.21	4.35	1.79	3.62	5.50	8.74	15.10	11.14	77.93
3	20	2.48	3.37	2.91	5.38	9.15	8.53	5.12	8.51	7.38	7.69	8.47	4.22	73.20
4	17	2.86	3.29	2.87	4.90	9.13	7.83	5.65	6.32	10.60	8.40	9.20	4.61	75.65
5	15	5.93	5.51	4.85	6.87	8.52	5.22	4.13	4.15	6.24	7.90	14.85	7.00	81.16
6	26	4.59	4.37	4.04	3.24	5.83	3.64	1.42	1.78	3.85	8.17	11.92	7.02	54.97
7	6	2.71	3.55	5.19	5.23	7.13	2.45	1.91	3.00	5.16	4.44	13.34	4.60	61.00
8	15	3.70	3.38	3.83	4.24	7.43	4.14	2.82	3.15	5.54	5.38	10.67	3.60	57.87
9	5	2.49	2.52	2.36	3.48	6.04	6.31	3.60	4.01	6.48	6.07	8.95	4.56	56.98
10	4	1.34	1.57	1.98	4.70	5.65	5.38	0.98	2.75	4.61	2.19	7.10	1.30	39.63
11	5	0.60	3.43	2.70	4.72	6.46	6.28	1.14	2.62	3.39	4.04	8.10	2.49	46.34
12	15	1.39	1.46	1.35	3.05	8.04	6.63	4.33	4.93	8.11	5.26	5.91	1.26	51.71
13†	4	4.40	3.65	3.18	3.75	13.78	14.04	7.92	7.54	11.21	7.61	11.25	5.17	83.50
14	34	2.61	2.52	3.00	3.86	7.04	4.33	2.78	4.20	6.14	5.64	7.94	4.08	54.15
15	8	1.36	0.59	2.04	2.03	5.67	6.31	4.58	5.56	6.52	8.44	4.31	2.76	50.17
16	9	2.43	1.61	2.52	4.20	6.52	4.57	4.00	3.97	5.29	6.62	6.88	5.47	52.10
17	9	0.79	0.74	0.74	3.57	4.80	5.31	3.85	3.45	4.26	3.26	2.31	0.61	34.23
18	15	0.62	0.82	2.00	4.40	7.20	5.43	3.74	4.88	5.20	5.36	2.32	0.41	42.38
					Mean Temperature in Degrees Fahrenheit								
2	6	72.3	72.4	73.6	75.8	77.4	78.9	80.2	80.2	79.9	78.9	76.2	73.5	76.6
6	6	75.0	73.2	75.2	77.4	78.6	79.2	80.6	79.0	80.8	81.5	78.3	76.8	77.9
7	5	73.2	73.4	74.5	76.3	78.3	78.4	79.9	79.9	80.2	81.7	78.3	74.8	77.4
8	7	73.4	73.0	73.9	77.4	77.9	79.2	79.5	79.9	80.1	79.5	76.6	73.8	77.0
15	1	70.5	70.9	74.5	75.9	77.0	79.0	79.5	79.3	79.9	78.4	74.8	70.9	75.9
					Mean Maximum Temperature in Degrees Fahrenheit								
2	6	79.3	79.9	81.3	83.1	84.7	86.7	88.3	88.3	88.0	86.7	83.3	80.4	84.2
6	7	79.9	79.3	80.4	82.0	84.4	86.4	86.7	87.4	87.4	85.5	82.4	80.2	83.5
					Mean Minimum Temperature in Degrees Fahrenheit								
2	6	65.3	64.9	65.8	68.4	70.2	71.1	72.0	72.1	71.8	71.1	69.1	66.6	69.0
6	7	66.9	66.7	67.8	69.6	71.4	73.0	73.6	73.8	73.9	72.1	70.5	68.7	70.7
					Maximum Rainfall in 24 Hours, in Inches								
6	14	4.57	7.32	7.10	3.23	3.00	2.27	2.20	4.25	3.75	5.96	6.28	9.04	9.04
					Mean Monthly Number of Days with Rain								
2	14	13	10	9	10	12	10	6	7	12	15	17	14	135
6	14	6	6	5	5	8	5	4	3	6	10	11	7	76

Maximum Rainfall in 24 Hours, in Inches

Pilate	9.06	Nov. 21, 1927	Bonnay	8.00	Nov. 30, 1931
Limbé	15.28	Nov. 21, 1927	Limonade	9.84	Sept. 14, 1928
Cap Haitien	15.04	Nov. 13, 1932			

Mean Annual Number of Days with Rain

Le Borgne	116	Cap Haitien	76	Grande Rivière	75
Pilate	100	Bonnay	96	St. Raphaël	67
Plaisance	129	Limonade	90	Cerca la Source	84
Limbé	112	Ounamenthe	76		

*Statistics from Leo Alpert, "Climate."
†Precipitation values given for this station are not in harmony with the land use picture, the verbal accounts given the author by residents of the area as to the length of the dry season, or the general pattern of climates in the Département. Since, also, the period of record is very short, these values have not been used in the delineation of climatic regions.

C. ANALYSES AND POTENTIAL YIELDS OF SOILS

1. Results of chemical soil analyses made in the Dept. of Agriculture, Port-au-Prince, Haiti

Soil type	Depth of sample	Horizon*	pH	Nitrates p.p.m.	Phosphorus lbs/acre	Potassium lbs/acre	Electrical conductivity
Gs	24"	C	7.4	16	50	40	0.7
Gs	Surf.	A	8.0	16	75	100	0.3
Ql	14"	B	7.8	16	50	40	0.2
Vy	Surf.	A	7.8	12	50	100	0.3
Vy	27"	C	8.0	16	25	40	0.1
Vl	Surf.	A	7.4	12	50	40	0.25
Vl	15"	B	8.0	14	25	40	0.3
Vl	30"	C	6.8	16	25	360	0.25
Bm	Surf.	A	7.8	12	75	40	0.6
Bm	16"	B	8.1	12	25	40	0.45
Ss	Surf.	—	7.2	12	200	40	0.4
Sd	24"	B	7.4	12	100	40	0.4
Sd	Surf.	A	8.1	12	200	360	0.3
Sd	24"	B	8.0	14	50	360	0.35
Lh	Surf.	—	7.6	16	100	360	1.1
Lp	Surf.	A	7.8	14	25	40	0.25
Lp	Surf.	—	7.8	16	100	80	0.25
Hd	Surf.	A	7.8	14	200	360	0.4
Hd	Surf.	A	8.0	14	75	100	0.1
Hd	Surf.	A	8.0	16	25	360	0.6
Hd	Surf.	A	7.8	14	200	100	0.7
Hd	Surf.	A	7.6	16	100	40	0.8
H	30"	C	8.0	16	25	40	0.35
H	20"	C	8.0	16	50	150	0.9
H	24"	C	7.8	10	25	40	0.4
Cg	24"	C	7.2	12	25	40	0.4
Cm	36"	C	7.2	10	25	40	3.4
Cm	Surf.	A	7.8	14	200	40	0.5
Cm	24"	B	7.6	14	150	40	0.3
Rm	70"	C	7.8	12	25	40	1.5
Uclw	Surf.	A	8.0	16	200	220	0.5
Uclw	Surf.	A	7.6	14	200	360	0.6
Ucli	Surf.	A	7.6	16	200	40	0.7
Ucli	Surf.	A	8.0	12	75	40	0.3
Us-c	15"	D	8.1	12	25	100	1.2
Usil	24"	B	7.6	14	150	40	0.35
Usil	Surf.	A	7.6	14	200	360	0.35
Ul-sis	Surf.	A	7.8	14	200	360	0.4
Ul-sis	Surf.	A	7.8	12	150	40	0.45
Usl-s	Surf.	A	7.6	12	150	80	0.3
Usy	Surf.	A	7.8	14	200	40	0.35
Usy	Surf.	A	7.6	12	150	100	0.7
Usy	Surf.	A	7.6	12	150	100	0.7
Usy	Surf.	A	7.2	14	200	360	0.25
Usm	Surf.	A	8.0	14	200	360	0.4
Ubr	Surf.	—	7.6	16	75	40	0.2
Ubr	24"	C	7.6	12	50	40	0.4
Uc-b	Surf.	A	7.6	12	200	40	0.4
Pf	Surf.	A	7.6	12	200	360	0.5
Pf	Surf.	A	7.2	12	200	360	0.35
Pc	Surf.	—	7.8	12	150	40	0.5
Fs	Surf.	—	7.8	16	200	360	0.5
Ts	24"	B	7.8	14	25	40	0.25

*A dash appearing in this column indicates that there is little or no differentiation between the surface materials and the underlying unconsolidated material.

2. Results of chemical soil analyses made in the Dept. of Geography,
McMaster University, Hamilton, Ont.

Soil type	Depth of sample	Horizon	pH	Nitrates p.p.m.	Phosphorus lbs/acre	Potassium lbs/acre
Gm	24″	C	5.2	1	85	110
Gm	30″	C	7.0	24	170	100
Gm	30″	C	6.8	1	75	130
Qw	Surf.	A	6.6	2.5	65	140
Qw	12″	B	6.0	1	100	120
Qw	24″	B	6.6	1	100	120
Qw	24″	C	6.4	1	65	160
Qw	8″	B	6.5	28	75	120
Vy	8″	A	6.6	1	75	110
Vl	36″	C	5.2	24	5	100
Bm	45″	C	8.0	28	15	120
Bm	18″	C	7.1	2.5	100	130
Bm	72″	Dr	7.0	4	50	95
Bm	12″	B	7.4	24	75	160
Sd	30″	Dr	4.6	20	65	300
Sd	25″	B	6.0	4	150	160
Sd	21″	C	5.0	1	40	130
Sd	25″	B	5.4	6	65	140
Sd	18″	B	5.0	12	75	120
Sd	6″	C	4.8	8	25	140
Sd	20″	C	6.8	1	75	180
Sd	30″	C	6.6	1	100	140
Lp	15″	B	5.0	1	100	150
Lp	24″	C	7.3	10	75	140
Hd	20″	C	7.0	1	75	140
Hd	21″	B	7.0	1	150	130
Hd	18″	B	5.6	1	150	120
Hd	Surf.	A	7.4	4	150	270
Hd	24″	C	7.4	1	25	170
Rs	Surf.	—	7.2	8	200	220
Rm	15″	C	7.0	24	10	120
Rm	24″	C	8.0	1	25	140
Uc	28″	C	7.6	2.5	65	140
Uc	72″	C	7.6	1	200	120
Uc	30″	C	7.0	1	170	130
Ucli	Surf.	A	6.8	1	200	120
Ucli	21″	B	7.0	1	150	110
Ucli	24″	A	7.4	1	170	120
Ucli	24″	C	7.0	6	150	150
Ucli	18″	C	6.4	2.5	60	120
Ucli	30″	C	7.4	1	75	120
Usi	18″	B	6.2	4	150	140
Usil	30″	C	7.6	12	50	40
Usil	24″	C	7.1	1	85	120
Usil	16″	A	5.0	12	75	110
Usil	21″	B	7.0	1	150	130
Ul-sis	20″	B	7.5	14	85	120
Usl-s	Surf.	A	6.2	14	200	180
Usl-s	30″	C	6.2	8	150	180
Usl-s	60″	C	6.8	1	100	160
Usy	Surf.	A	6.8	1	100	160
Usy	30″	C	6.3	6	50	120
Usy	48″	B	7.0	2.4	100	110
Usy	12″	B	8.1	12	25	100
Ubr	10″	A₂	6.4	1	125	160
Ubr	84″	C	7.0	2.5	60	100
Uc-b	Surf.	A	7.0	1	100	120
Pf	36″	C	7.0	1	50	120
Pc	20″	C	6.7	1	65	120

3. Results of mechanical soil analysis made in the Dept. of Agriculture, Port-au-Prince, Haiti

Soil type	Depth of sample	Horizon	Water† capacity	Percentage org. matter	Percentage sand	Percentage silt	Percentage clay
Gs	24″	C	34	0	60	10	30
Gs	Surf.	A	40	1.92	53.97	21.76	22.35
Ql	14″	B	47	0	50	34	16
Vy	Surf.	A	40	3.78	56.04	20.11	20.07
Vy	27″	C	51	0	44	40	16
Vl	Surf.	A	53	23.86	36.38	31.62	8.14
Vl	30″	C	52	0	32	36	32
Bm	Surf.	A	51	8.80	32.70	40.15	18.35
Bm	16″	B	50	0	34	44	22
Ss	Surf.	—	50	6.03	45.28	34.51	14.18
Sd	24″	B	47	0	44	38	18
Sd	Surf.	A	40	0	48	20	32
Sd	24″	B	70	0	20	64	16
Lh	Surf.	—	60	3.41	35.10	33.03	25.15
Lp	Surf.	A	60	0	46	38	16
Lp	Surf.	—	40	14.15	40.62	28.15	17.08
Hd	Surf.	A	49	18.37	16.32	49.20	16.11
Hd	Surf.	A	60	21.49	14.08	44.17	20.26
Hd	Surf.	A	40	0	44	40	16
Hd	Surf.	A	40	15.10	50.33	15.92	18.65
Hd	Surf.	A	39	23.21	34.19	20.53	22.17
H	30″	C	40	0	44	18	38
H	21″	C	56	0	26	58	18
H	24″	C	40	0	24	20	56
Cm	Surf.	A	41	0	46	32	22
Cm	36″	C	61	0	40	48	12
Uclw	Surf.	A	56	9.53	28.07	22.27	40.13
Uclw	Surf.	A	48	3.89	40.11	24.82	31.18
Ucli	Surf.	A	53	7.29	24.16	20.37	48.18
Ucli	Surf.	A	45	0	28	28	44
Usil	24″	B	52	0	24	24	52
Usil	Surf.	A	49	6.03	40.32	28.47	25.18
Usl-s	Surf.	A	45	3.88	45.12	24.65	26.35
Usy	Surf.	A	64	0	28	22	50
Usy	Surf.	A	46	4.73	23.65	22.58	49.04
Usy	Surf.	A	40	0	64	8	28
Usm	Surf.	A	33	3.98	68.07	17.68	10.27
Ubr	Surf.	—	44	6.64	40.22	16.04	37.10
Pf	Surf.	A	63	0	54	18	28
Pc	Surf.	—	36	2.25	45.35	26.52	24.14
Fs	Surf.	—	52	0	42	28	30
Ts	24″	B	40	0	58	30	12

†Water capacity is the number of c.c. of water required to saturate 100 grams of soil, and indicates the degree of permeability of the soil.

D. PRODUCTIVITY RATINGS FOR PUERTO RICAN AND SIMILAR HAITIAN SOILS*
(from R. C. Roberts, *Soil Survey of Puerto Rico*)

Haiti soil	Puerto Rico soil†	Sugar cane	Tobacco	Coffee	Grapefruit	Pineapples	Bananas	Corn	Sweet potato	Peas & beans	Yam	Coconuts	Cotton	Hay	Pasture	General Rating
Gs	Pandura SCL	—	45	50	—	—	40	30	35	30	—	—	—	—	25	6
Gs	Ciales CL	40	50	70	—	—	50	30	40	40	—	—	—	—	25	6
Gs	Teja L	30	40	—	—	—	30	15	45	35	—	60	—	—	15	8
Gm	Las Piedras CL	60	75	—	70	70	65	70	60	40	—	60	—	30	65	4
Qw	Vieques L	20	40	—	—	—	—	15	20	20	—	—	—	—	25	8
Ql	Sayuya SiCL	45	50	60	—	—	65	35	50	40	40	—	—	20	25	6
Qyl	Cialitos C	40	20	50	60	60	60	15	35	30	35	—	—	—	30	7
Vy	Mucara SiCL	30	45	50	—	—	50	45	20	65	70	—	—	—	50	7
Vy	Juncos C	60	70	60	—	—	70	65	35	75	—	—	—	20	60	4
Vl	Catalina C	50	25	70	70	75	70	15	50	30	40	—	—	15	30	5
By	Sabana SiCL	25	40	45	—	—	55	30	25	60	—	—	—	—	45	8
Bm	Naranjito SiL	30	40	55	—	—	60	25	20	50	—	—	—	—	35	7
Bm	Guayama C	15	—	—	—	—	—	35	15	—	—	—	—	—	25	10
St	Descalabrado SiC Shallow Phase	—	—	—	—	—	—	—	5	15	—	—	—	—	50	10
Ss	Descalabrado SiC	—	—	—	—	—	—	—	10	—	—	—	—	—	25	10
Ss	Yunes Clay	—	—	45	—	—	60	—	25	—	—	—	—	—	25	8
Sd	Rio Piedras C	50	—	60	30	30	70	45	25	40	40	—	—	—	25	5
Lh	Tanama Stony C	—	—	10	—	—	25	—	20	10	10	—	—	—	15	10
Lh	Lajas C	—	15	15	—	—	30	—	20	15	—	—	—	—	15	10
Lhd	Colinas CL	60	60	—	—	—	40	45	30	90	—	—	—	40	40	4
Lp	Ensenada C	—	—	—	—	—	5	5	5	5	—	—	—	—	56	10
Lp	Coto C	80	45	—	50	—	55	50	50	50	150	—	—	—	50	3
Hd	Purtugués C	100	—	—	—	—	65	90	—	—	—	—	—	—	35	2
Hd	Camagüey SiC	75	75	80	20	—	80	100	40	90	60	—	—	60	75	3
H	Soller C	75	60	50	—	—	75	100	25	90	—	—	—	—	70	3
H	Santa Clara CL	75	50	—	—	—	85	90	35	80	—	—	—	55	80	3
Cm	Plata C	55	50	—	—	—	65	45	20	60	—	—	—	—	30	5
Uc	Caguas C	55	50	—	30	55	50	30	25	40	—	—	—	60	50	5
Uclw	Islote CL	65	50	—	80	—	60	50	95	65	60	85	60	—	40	4
Ucli	Martin Peña C	70	—	—	—	—	—	—	—	100	—	—	—	100	90	4
Us-c	Vega Alta Fine SL	30	30	—	60	—	45	15	95	40	—	—	60	—	50	6
Usi	San Antón SiC	150	—	—	—	—	—	—	—	—	—	—	—	—	—	1
Usil	Altura SiL	150	—	—	—	—	—	—	—	—	—	—	—	—	—	1
Usil	Coloso SiL	105	—	—	—	—	—	—	—	—	—	—	—	100	150	1
Ufs	Corozo Fine S	—	—	—	15	30	20	—	25	10	—	15	40	—	10	10
Usy	Aguadilla SL	30	—	—	90	60	40	15	100	70	30	100	90	—	45	6
Usm	Maleza LS	35	30	—	95	—	70	30	100	40	—	60	50	—	30	7
Ub	Palm Beach S	—	—	—	—	—	30	—	30	30	—	60	—	—	30	10
Uc-b	Corcega SL	50	—	—	65	—	50	—	100	80	—	75	—	60	55	5
Uss	Meros S, Saline	—	—	—	—	—	—	—	15	—	—	—	—	—	20	10
Wf	Tiburones Muck	40	—	—	—	—	—	—	—	—	—	—	—	60	60	10
Wm	Ursula C	—	—	—	—	—	—	—	—	—	—	—	—	—	25	10
Pf	Vives CL	95	—	—	—	—	—	—	—	—	—	—	—	—	—	1
Fsi	Toa SiL	115	100	—	—	—	—	—	—	—	—	—	—	—	—	1
Fs	Estación L	70	90	80	—	—	85	95	75	85	100	—	—	110	60	3
Fs	Viví L	75	100	100	—	—	85	60	80	60	—	—	—	—	—	4

*An index rating of 100 equals the following yields per acre after the land has been drained where necessary and in dry areas irrigated:

100 tons sugar cane	6000 lbs. sweet potatoes
1800 lbs. tobacco	500 lbs. peas or beans
600 lbs. coffee	8000 lbs. yam
600 boxes grapefruit	6000 lbs. coconuts
500 crates pineapples	1000 lbs. cotton
60,000 fingers bananas	20 tons hay
2000 lbs. corn	700 cow-acre days.

†The following abbreviations are used in this column: C—Clay; Si—Silt; L—Loam; S—Sand.

E. CHARACTERISTICS OF PLANTS COMMONLY CULTIVATED
IN THE DÉPARTEMENT DU NORD

Bananas and Plantains

These tree-like herbaceous plants so closely resemble each other that only an expert can distinguish between them. The fruit of the former, however, is edible raw while that of the latter must be cooked. The plants are quick-growing, and the fruit is produced in thirteen to sixteen months for new plantings and up to twenty-four months for old ones. Propagation is by suckers.

Temperatures for optimum growth must not fall below 73.4° F., and 80″ of rain, well-distributed throughout the year, is desirable. Adequate moisture is particularly necessary during the tenth to the fifth month before the harvest. Soils should be rich, deep, well-drained, and rather light-textured with adequate supplies of lime and humus. Salinity, even in a slight degree, is particularly harmful.

Beans and Peas

Several types of beans are grown in the Département, but the only common pea is the chick pea. These are all annuals requiring, in general, average temperatures of 80° during a growing season of three to six months. A wide variety of soils is suitable, and soil fertility is seldom a limiting factor in production. Indeed, high fertility is a disadvantage. Soil texture should be fairly light and there should be a uniform supply of moisture during the vegetative period.

Cacao

This tree of humid tropical lowlands produces, upon its trunk and larger branches, large pods which contain the cacao beans. It is very sensitive to drought, cold, and wind. Temperatures must not fall below 60°, and uniform precipitation with 60″ to 190″ of rain per year is desirable. The plant is quite tolerant of salinity in the soils, but needs fairly abundant supplies of potash and nitrogen as well as moderate amounts of phosphorus. There should also be a high content of humus in the soil. The plant is seldom grown at elevations exceeding 1500 feet.

Coffee

This is a large bush or low tree producing beans along its branches. The beans do not usually all ripen at the same time, and, in the Département, they are picked by hand and dried in the sun. Coffee is normally started in nurseries and then transplanted to the fields. Yields commence after the third or fourth year, reach a maximum during the sixth to the tenth years, and cease to be profitable after about the thirtieth year.

Too much light is harmful to the trees, and they are usually grown under shade. Optimum temperatures are 60° to 78°, and 50″ to 90″ of rain are needed, preferably well-distributed, but with a fairly dry period in the harvest season. Soils should be loamy, deep, well-drained, rich in humus, and preferably with a reaction between pH 5.0 and 6.0. Fairly large quantities of nitrogen and potash are required.

Corn

Types of corn commonly grown in Haiti require three to four and a half months to reach maturity. The relatively slow rate of deterioration of the grain when stored on the cob increases its importance as a Haitian food crop.

Temperatures above 78° are needed for high yields of corn and there should be abundant moisture (18″ to 24″) during the growing season, though drier conditions are desirable during the ripening of the grain. Soils should be well drained and well aerated, with abundant supplies of nitrates. Loams and silt loams well supplied with humus are ideal. The plant tolerates easily a range in soil reaction from pH 5.5 to 8.0.

Guinea Grass

A bunch grass with a vertical habit of growth, this plant may reach a height of four to six feet in Haiti. It is often pastured, but, if it is cut, four to eight cuttings may be made annually. It is propagated by division of the roots, and once planted it regenerates even though the land is burned over and planted for a year or so in another crop.

A wide variety of soils is suitable, provided they are well drained, and the plant is able to survive periods of drought. However, the leaves become desiccated during prolonged dry weather and are then unsuitable as feed for cattle.

Manioc

A low bush, six to ten feet in height, manioc is a prolific producer of tubers, rich in starch but low in protein, fat, and vitamins. Propagation is by cuttings. In Haiti the tubers require eighteen months to two years to mature, but may be left in the ground for a longer period without deterioration to be dug up when needed. Once removed from the ground, however, the tubers must be used immediately. They are commonly ground into flour and made into a coarse bread.

The plant requires high temperatures and abundant sunshine, but is able to stand rather intense and prolonged drought. Fertile soils, rich in potash, produce the highest yields, but manioc also produces well on leached soils. Light soil texture is desirable, and good drainage is essential to prevent the tubers rotting.

Rice

Both paddy and upland rice are produced in the Département, the former requiring four to six months, the latter six to seven months to mature. Rice must have temperatures not less than 60° to 68° and at least 40″ rain a year. The need for water increases from planting time to the middle of the vegetative period and then declines. For paddy rice some clay in the subsoil is essential, but upland rice will grow in sandy or lateritic soils. Slightly acid soil (pH 5.6–6.5) is best, but the plant is very tolerant of differences in reaction. It is also one of the least soil-exhausting of all crops.

Rubber

The hevea tree, which is the only plant currently producing rubber in the

Département, may be tapped for latex after the fifth year and, if carefully treated, has a long productive life. The tree requires temperatures between a mean minimum of 75° and a mean maximum of 95°, and there should be over 70″ of rain evenly distributed throughout the year. Good drainage is essential and deep alluvial soils are best. Soils should be rich in nitrogen and also contain moderate supplies of phosphorus and potassium.

Sisal

Sisal is a stemless perennial with stiff, thick, fleshy leaves four to six feet long and three to five inches in width. The fibre content of the leaves, by weight, is about 3 per cent in humid and 4 per cent in dry areas; in the former, however, growth is more rapid. Harvesting, which consists of cutting off the leaves, begins when the plant is three and a half to four years old and continues at intervals of six months to a year until the age of the plant is seven to eight years. The fibre may be extracted by hand, but, for commercial production, machinery is necessary.

Sisal is very hardy, extremely drought-resistant, and does not require very fertile soils.

Sugar Cane

This perennial rank-growing grass may reach a height of ten to fourteen feet and a diameter of two to two and a half inches. It is propagated by cuttings, the first crop ripening in fifteen to twenty-four months and subsequent, or ratoon, crops in about a year. The juice is extracted by passing the cane between steel rollers, and it is essential that processing be carried out very shortly after harvesting to prevent fermentation.

Optimum temperature for growth is about 90°, but, for commercial production, lower temperatures during the ripening period are desirable. Abundant moisture is needed (50″–65″ per year), especially during the period of vegetative growth, but it is important that there should be a dry ripening period. Soils must be of high fertility, deep, friable and well drained, yet able to retain moisture. A loamy texture and slight alkalinity of the soil are preferred, though the plant can tolerate moderately acid conditions.

Sweet Potatoes

This vine produces edible tubers which mature four to seven months after planting, but which deteriorate rather quickly after maturing and are not easily stored. Consequently, to stretch out the harvest, peasants in the Département commonly commence digging up the tubers after about three months, when they are edible, but not yet of maximum size.

The plant requires high temperatures and abundant sunshine, but is fairly tolerant of dry weather. It is also lenient with respect to soil requirements; high fertility is undesirable as it results in poor root development. The soils should, however, be friable, warm and well drained, a sandy topsoil with heavier subsoil being particularly suitable.

Taro

Called also eddo, dasheen, and yautia, this is a coarse herbaceous plant with large shield-shaped leaves. It bears spherical starchy tubers which mature in eight to fourteen months, and is propagated by suckers. Like rice, taro exists in both paddy and upland varieties, but only the latter is common in the Département.

High temperatures and high rainfall with little or no dry season are required. The plant also prefers soils of moderate texture but is tolerant of low fertility.

Bibliography

REFERENCES DEALING SPECIFICALLY WITH HAITI

ALPERT, LEO, "The Climate of Hispaniola," Clark University, Worcester, Mass., M.A. thesis, 1939.
BUTTERLIN, J., *La Géologie de la République d'Haiti*, Memoires de l'Institut Francais d'Haiti, No. 1 (Port-au-Prince, 1954).
DALENCOUR, F., *Histoire de la Nation Haitienne* (Port-au-Prince, 1930).
EATON, F. M., *Land Development of the Artibonite Plain of Haiti* (New York: United Nations, 1952).
HOLLY, M. A., *Agriculture in Haiti* (New York, 1955).
Bulletins Trimestriel de Statistique (Port-au-Prince: Institut Haitien de Statistique).
Recensement Général, août 1950 (Port-au-Prince: Institut Haitien de Statistique).
PEREIRA, P., *Géographie d'Haiti* (Port-au-Prince, 1938).
PRESSOIR, C. and TROUILLOT, H., *l'Enseignement de la Géographie en Haiti*, Pan-American Institute of Geography and History, Publication 197–I (Rio de Janeiro, 1955).
Mission to Haiti, Publication IIb.2 (Lake Success: United Nations, 1949).
WOOD, H. A., "Stream Piracy in the Central Plateau of Hispaniola," *The Canadian Geographer*, no. 8, 1956, pp. 46–54.
WOOD, H. A., "Physical Influences on Peasant Agriculture in Northern Haiti," *The Canadian Geographer*, vol. V(2), 1961, pp. 10–18.
WOODRING, W. P., BROWN, J. A., and BURBANK, W. S., *Geology of the Republic of Haiti* (Port-au-Prince, 1954).

GENERAL REFERENCES

KLAGES, K. H. W., *Ecological Crop Geography* (New York, 1947).
MOHR, E. C. J. and VAN BAREN, F. A., *Tropical Soils* (The Hague, 1954).
ROBERTS, R. C., *Soil Survey of Puerto Rico*, United States Department of Agriculture, Bur. Plant Ind. Ser. 1936, no. 8, 1942.
TANNEHILL, I. R., *Hurricanes* (Princeton, 1945).
Soil Survey Manual, United States Department of Agriculture Handbook no. 18 (Washington, 1951).
VAN ROYEN, W., *The Agricultural Resources of the World* (New York, 1954).
WILCOX, E. V., *Tropical Agriculture* (New York, 1916).

Index